That Kind of Girl

A Girl's Bible Study

by

Katy Leigh Foster

A King David Kind of Girl
A Girl's Bible Study
by Katy Leigh Foster

All rights reserved. No part of this book may be reproduced or transmitted in any form or by any means, electronic or mechanical, including photocopying, recording or by any information storage and retrieval system, without written permission from the author, except for the inclusion of brief quotations in a review, or for the expanding of God's kingdom through Jesus Christ.

Copyright ©2023 by Katy Foster
Printed by KDP, Seattle, Washington, United States
All rights reserved.

ISBN 13: 979-8851353567

Scripture taken from the New King James Version®. Copyright © 1982 by Thomas Nelson. Used by permission.

Licensed and permission granted for the following fonts by Kimberly Geswein: "KG Flavor and Frames," "KG Flavor and Frames 6," "KG True Colors," "KG Heart Doodles," and "Janda Cheerful Script."
Permission also granted through Fontspace for "Princess and the Frog" by Esteban4058, and for "DuCahier" by Philippe Tassel.
"Bow and arrows" photograph by deathunicorn through Morguefile.
Cover photograph by Scott Liddell, "hotblack" through Morguefile.

All other images were created by the author with all rights reserved as stated above.

Printed in the United States of America.

A King David Kind of Girl

A Girl's Bible Study

by

Katy Leigh Foster

For of Him and through Him and to Him are all things to whom be glory forever. Amen.

Romans 11:36

Table of Contents

Intro: Your First Step — 1
The Light: See, Study, Understand
The Lamp: The LORD, Our Shepherd

Chapter 1: Let's Dig In — 1 Samuel 16:1-13; Psalm 23 — 5
Lesson 1: Meet Samuel
Lesson 2: Heart It!
Lesson 3: A Youngster
Lesson 4: The LORD, Our Shepherd

Chapter 2: Our Dear Dad — 1 Samuel 16:14-23 — 15
Lesson 1: A God of Light
Lesson 2: Sing It, Sister!
Lesson 3: Acceptance

Chapter 3: Along the Way — 1 Samuel 17 — 21
Lesson 1: A Big Problem
Lesson 2: Mom & Dad
Lesson 3: Hello!
Lesson 4: You've Got This!

Chapter 4: Friends — 1 Samuel 18:1-14; 1 Corinthians 13:4-7 — 31
Lesson 1: BFFs
Lesson 2: How to Love My Friends
Lesson 3: Instigators

Chapter 5: A Strong Second — 1 Sam 18:15 to 20:11; Psalm 70 & 84 — 37
Lesson 1: Humility
Lesson 2: One More Thing, God
Lesson 3: The Power of Fellowship
Lesson 4: Please Understand
Lesson 5: The Comfort of Church
Lesson 6: There's No Place Like Church
Lesson 7: Your Servant

Chapter 6: All Those Around Me — 1 Samuel 20:12-42 to 22:4 — 49
Lesson 1: Be a Later-Hater
Lesson 2: Jonathan
Lesson 3: The Truth
Lesson 4: My Fab Fam

Chapter 7: Growing UP — 1 Samuel 22:5 to 24:16 — 59
Lesson 1: A Heart Apart
Lesson 2: God's Take
Lesson 3: Good Talk

Lesson 4: So Encouraging!
Lesson 5: He's Got the Whole World!
Lesson 6: Nature Calls

Chapter 8: My Teacher   1 Samuel 24:17 to 25; Psalm 57   69
Lesson 1: Be Inspiring!
Lesson 2: Tough Times
Lesson 3: Giving
Lesson 4: The Beautiful Abigail

Chapter 9: Closer and Closer   1 Sam 26 to 28:6; Psalm 37:1-8   77
Lesson 1: Night Night
Lesson 2: All For You, God!
Lesson 3: Listen
Lesson 4: Wild Heart
Lesson 5: Peace It Together
Lesson 6: You There, God?

Chapter 10: Woman-Practice   1 Sam 28:7, 1 Sam 29 to 30:6;   89
Psalm 5:11-12; Psalm 8
Lesson 1: Don't Be Scared
Lesson 2: Set Apart
Lesson 3: A Way to Help
Lesson 4: Loneliness
Lesson 5: Something to Remember

Chapter 11: Your Bible   1 Samuel 30:7-20; 1 Chronicles 12:16-18;   101
Psalm 13
Lesson 1: The Believers
Lesson 2: Our Helper
Lesson 3: Your Strength
Lesson 4: The Bad Days

Chapter 12: Words of Life   1 Samuel 30:21-31; 2 Samuel 1; Psalm 67   109
Lesson 1: "Stew"ing Over
Lesson 2: A Sad Ending
Lesson 3: A Rough Start
Lesson 4: The Good Side
Lesson 5: It's You, God!

Chapter 13: Our Father   2 Samuel 2, 3:1-5; Psalm 63; Romans 5:3-5   121
Lesson 1: Here I Am, God
Lesson 2: David Makes History
Lesson 3: Hold On!
Lesson 4: The Struggle
Lesson 5: Let's Meet Our Contestants
Lesson 6: A Message
Lesson 7: The Truth

Chapter 14: Seek His Heart!   2 Samuel 3:6-4; 5:1-10,   135
Psalm 119:1-24
Lesson 1: A Delight
Lesson 2: Shhh!
Lesson 3: Time for Work
Lesson 4: Down Low

Lesson 5: The Two Paths
Lesson 6: The Journey Continues

Memory Verses   151
Maps   156

Your First Step

Studying the life of David will not turn you into a fierce manly warrior. You won't grow a beard or feel the need to savagely eat a turkey leg and laugh loudly with a mouth full of food. You shouldn't, anyway. God created you to be a girl, and as you study the life of David, a girl you will stay. However, there will be some changes going on in your life. You will know God more, and *this* will forever change your whole life. He has some wonderful things to show you. When you know God more, you'll know yourself more, because God will show you what an amazing young woman He created.

David is known as "a man after God's own heart." God wants us to know Him completely, which means knowing His heart. It's like knowing a best friend. You may know where she lives, her name, and her age; but you also know what she likes, and what she doesn't like. You know what is in her heart!

You may know that our Heavenly Father resides in heaven. You may know Him as the Creator; but do you know what He likes, what He loves, what He dislikes, and what He hates? Do you know what makes God smile, and what breaks His heart? Do you want to search for God's heart, as David did?...

Your first step should be taken with your Bible, opened in your hands. We need to read this big love letter that He wrote to us. As you search for God's heart by reading your Bible, God will draw your heart closer to His own.

The Lamp
See, Study, Understand

In **Psalm 119:18**, David says, *"Open my eyes that I may see Wondrous things from Your law."*

God can show us exactly what He wants us to see and know in the Bible. Each time you open your Bible, pause and ask God to help you read it.

Look up and copy **Psalm 119:50** in the space provided.

_____

_____

Just as David, you can pray these same verses.

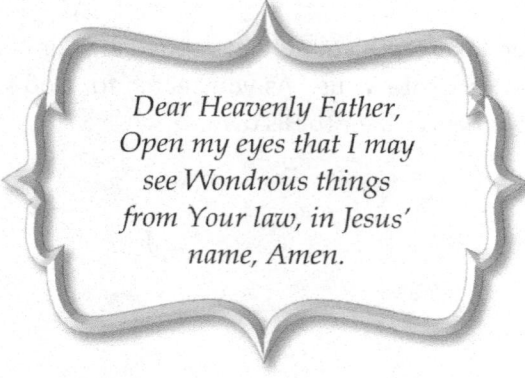

Dear Heavenly Father, Open my eyes that I may see Wondrous things from Your law, in Jesus' name, Amen.

The Light
Jesus

Second Corinthians 4:6 tells us,

*For it is the God who commanded light to
shine out of darkness,
who has shone in our hearts to give
the light of the knowledge*
of the glory of God in the face of Jesus Christ.

†

Jesus came to earth when He didn't have to. He lived among hurt, worry, darkness, and grief, and He didn't have to. He endured brutal beatings followed by torn flesh on the cross, although He did no wrong, and He didn't have to. He died in loneliness and in unimaginable pain, and He didn't have to.

For 33 years, with every breath He took, with every step He took, with every smile and with every frown He bore, He loved you. And He loves you, and He always will. He is the Light, and He shows us true love.

My dear precious sister, take the Light's hand and see --- God *is* love!

What? Where's Jesus' hand? Oh, look in your Bible. You'll find it there.

Chapter 1
Let's Dig In

When you pick up your Bible, it's nothing like you see on TV. No magical portals appear. Heavenly, God-given revelations appear, and no TV show can come close to just how divine and wonderful that is.

Your Bible is like no other book. No other book can change absolutely everything about your life like the Bible can. And if you'll pick it up and read it, you will find this out for yourself.

Lesson 1
Meet Samuel

A. In the land of Israel, the people known as the Israelites urged the godly priest Samuel to give them a king. Samuel had always been close to God, and he thought it was a bad idea to have any other king than God. He tried to explain to them that God alone was to be their king. However, the people pressed on.

God gave Samuel permission to anoint a man named Saul to be the first king. So, King Saul ruled Israel. However, King Saul did not walk with God in much of his decision-making as King. (Found in 1 Samuel 8, 9, and 10.) Samuel was sad about the whole thing, but God had plans for a new king...

Read **1 Samuel 16:1-5.**

Write a summary or your own thoughts of the reading:

_____
_____

B. God instructed Samuel to anoint a new king. See how Samuel responds. He took this task seriously by *sacrificing* first. Samuel instructed others that were coming to the sacrifice to "sanctify" themselves, and to "consecrate" themselves.

To *sanctify* ourselves is to cleanse our hearts of sin. ♡

Consecration is a separation from our normal routine. If some of our day doesn't involve God, then we just stay away from those things (TV, particular music, particular friends, ...).

How can you *sanctify* yourself?
_____

How can you *consecrate* yourself?
_____

What can you *sacrifice*?

_____

Share these plans with a family member or friend.

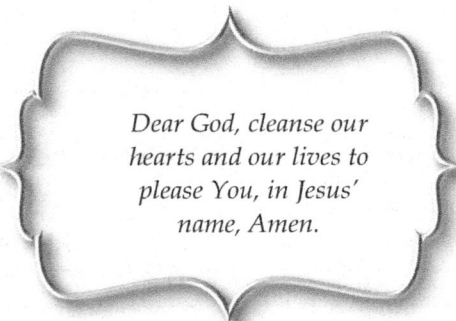

Dear God, cleanse our hearts and our lives to please You, in Jesus' name, Amen.

Lesson 2
Heart It!

𝒜. Read **1 Samuel 16:6-7**.

Write a summary or your own thoughts of the reading:

_____
_____

𝒲rite **1 Samuel 16:7b** ("b" means the second part of the verse) below, and memorize this verse:

_____
_____
_____
_____

ℬ. Do you spend more time on your *inner* appearance (your heart and mind) or your *outer* appearance?

How can we help our hearts look great? Jesus has the answer. He says in **Matthew 6:21,**

> For where your treasure is there your heart will be also.

Jesus also tells where our hearts should be: our hearts should be preparing for heaven.

We prepare for heaven by realizing that one day we will *all* see God's face. On that day, every single person in the world will get on their knees and worship God. And when His eyes meet yours, imagine how He gazes on you. So proud of His girl! You **listened** to Him and **trusted** Him, and even when it was difficult, you **obeyed** Him. This moment is what we are to focus on every day! Make this your treasure. Put your heart here!

In **Matthew 3:17**, God's triumphant voice resounded after Jesus was baptized, and said,

> "This is my beloved Son, in whom I am well pleased."

Wouldn't you love to hear God Almighty, the Creator, the King of all Kings, say to you, ...

> "This is my beloved daughter, in whom I am well pleased."

Place your heart here!

*Dear Heavenly Father,
Making YOU happy is
where
I want my heart,
in Jesus' name, Amen.*

Lesson 3
A Youngster

A. Read **1 Samuel 16:8-13**.

Write a summary or your own thoughts of the reading:

_____
_____

Can you imagine the anticipation? *Which son of Jesse will it be? .... What? David? Are you sure??*

David was the youngest, and he had the dirty work of watching the sheep. Yet, he was chosen to do God's work. Did God give any regard to age? No! *And God wants you to know this!*

B. The Bible talks about many people from history that were very young when they did God's work.

Samuel heard God's voice at a young age when he served Eli in the temple.

King Josiah became king of Israel when he was 8 years old.

Mary may have been as young as 14 when the angel Gabriel told her she would give birth to the Savior of the world.

Jesus was only 12 when He spoke with the teachers and scribes about the truths of the Old Testament.

Timothy was a very young man when he became a preacher.

How old are you? It's fun to think about what we want to do when we grow up; however, dear sister in Christ, you don't have to wait until you're older to do God's work. It is true that as you get older, you will become smarter and wiser, but today matters. There is something you can do for God today – read your Bible, choose kindness, choose honesty, choose forgiveness, be a helper, obey your parents, share God's love,…..

So, what kind of work for God would you like to do today?

_____

C. Look up **1 Timothy 4:12**, copy the verse below, and memorize:

_____
_____
_____

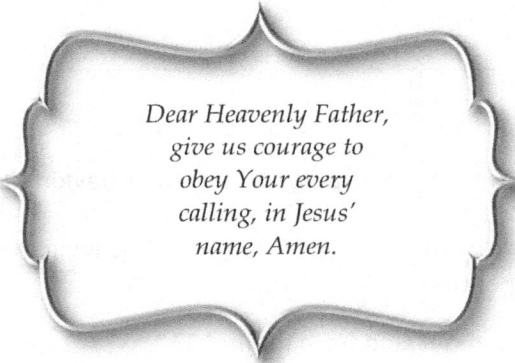

Dear Heavenly Father, give us courage to obey Your every calling, in Jesus' name, Amen.

Lesson 4
The LORD, Our Shepherd

A. Read **Psalm 23**.

Write a summary or your own thoughts of the reading:

_____
_____

What is a *Shepherd?* _____

B. David says God is his **Shepherd,** and then David tells us what our Heavenly Father does for us as He shepherds us. Just imagine, lying in soft green grass beside refreshing water – so peaceful!

What have you learned about God from Psalm 23?

_____
_____
_____

Share with a family member or a friend what you have learned about who God is from reading Psalm 23.

Chapter 2
Our Dear Dad

In 2016, the U.S. Census Bureau stated that 24 million children in the United States did not live with their biological father. Therefore, many children do not experience speaking and laughing with their dads every day. Many don't have the option to holler for Dad when there's a bug on the wall, or when something is too heavy to carry, or when something needs to be repaired. Consequently, many of us figure out life without Dad by our side.

Yet there's still a hunger for a father's protection and love. All children have that hunger. Some have a dad to fill that hunger; and many just don't. Maybe you don't. But for all of us girls, we have our Heavenly Father, who has a special place in His heart and in His plans for the fatherless.

In Jeremiah 33:3, God tells us, "Call to Me, and I will answer you, and show you great and mighty things, which you do not know." He gives us so much protection and love. He's a good Father.

God wants you to know Him, because He loves you. Have a special place in your heart for our Father. He says to you,

"Come to Me,…"

Lesson 1
A God of Light

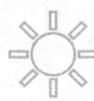

𝓐. Read **1 Samuel 16: 14-15**.

An evil spirit from the LORD... what???...

We want to know God more. That is why we read our Bibles. And, God our Father *wants* us to know Him more. We find out more about the heart of God by finding our answers in the Bible. There are other verses in the Bible that we can lean on in our search for God's heart. Read the following verse:

> "I form the light and create darkness,
> I make peace and create calamity;
> I, the LORD, do all these things.'
> Isaiah 45:7

Explain what this verse means to you.

_____
_____

𝓑. King Saul rarely sought God. Even in his distress, he *did not* seek God!

𝓝ow read **1 Samuel 16:14** again. Then, have prayer time with God, and write down your own explanation of this verse.

_____
_____
_____

Lesson 2
Sing It, Sister!

A. Read **1 Samuel 16:16-23**.

Write a summary or your own thoughts of the reading:

_____
_____

Saul and his servants did not know that David, the young man playing the harp, would one day be the king. They just saw David as a musician.

Music is a wonderful gift from God. Do you have a favorite praise song?

_____

B. Read **Psalm 150**, and explain how you can praise God with *music* this week:

_____
_____

> *Dear Heavenly Father,*
> *Thank You for music!*
> *How great Thou art! In Jesus'*
> *name, Amen!*

Using our gifts to glorify the Lord.
Romans 12:4-8

Lesson 3
Acceptance

A. Read **1 Samuel 16:23** (one more time, please).

As a young lady, there's something else very important about this verse. Notice that David did as he was told by authority. He played his harp. He made his music beautiful enough to relieve the king's stress.

The king did not know that the harp player would one day take his throne, or that he had already been anointed with oil from Samuel. But *David* knew.

Did David *tell anyone?* No!

Did David *cause drama?* No!

Did David *disrespect* King Saul, by saying things under his breath, perhaps like, "Enjoy it while you can,"? No!

David had the perfect opportunity to beam and glow, to take charge and be known. He could have boasted. He could have shined. He could have been on top of the world.

Yet, he simply obeyed the King, sat quietly, and played his harp.

Perhaps you have amazing talents or skills. Do you feel the need to shine before others, or to seek approval and acceptance from others?

Social media encourages us to glorify ourselves, and to look for approval from others. But that is *NEVER, EVER* God's plan!

Dear young woman, God made you to be so wonderful. If you have accepted Jesus as your Savior and Lord, you have been cleansed from all sin and made heir to the throne of the King of all kings! Along the way, as you are growing, God has provided you with special gifts and an unmatched power of the Holy Spirit. Be wise!

B. God is very proud of His daughters when they speak wisely and behave. How?

Look up **1 Peter 3:4** to see, and after reading the verse, write down how you think God wants you to behave:

_____

_____

Look up **Psalm 115:1**, copy the verse down below, and commit the verse to memory deep within your heart.

_____

_____

_____

_____

> *Dear Heavenly Father,*
> *Not unto us, but to Your name give glory,*
> *In Jesus' name, Amen.*

Chapter 3
Along the Way

I love to hike. Reaching the top of a mountain or a waterfall is a great reward after a long hike, but my favorite part about hiking is the path along the way. I love to hear water trickle down a stream as I walk beside it; or hear the water rush down a roaring river and waterfall where I can hardly hear my own voice. I love to stop and stare in wonder of the continuous flow of water that never stops. It helps me think of God as the Creator of what I see. The unstoppable flow of water reminds me, and overwhelms me, of God's relentless love that never stops. I love to catch a glimpse of a shy deer deep within the forest. I love to see the colors of the leaves, the height of the trees, and feel the peace of stillness around me.

Anywhere we go, there is a path to be taken. Even on the way to the dentist, or to school, we gaze out the window, we listen to the radio, and we have conversations. The path along the way is filled with a big part of our lives.

You are also taking a path into becoming a woman. Every second that passes is a gift from God, and we can see and learn so much along the way. Life is so wonderful.

Even though Jesus was born to die for us, He took an amazing path along the way of miracles and teaching and healing. Today is part of our journey. Let's make it an amazing, joyous journey along the way!

Lesson 1
A Big Problem

𝒜. Read **1 Samuel 17:1-7**.

Write a summary or your own thoughts of the reading:

_____
_____

A large open field lay flat, ending with mountains on opposite sides of the vast, flat land. The Philistine armies occupied one mountain, and on the other end of the valley was the Israelite army. The Israelites peered over to their opponents and saw one of the biggest men that they had ever seen -- Goliath! How big was he?

- *"six cubits and a span"* – This is approximately 9 feet 6 inches tall.
- *His coat of mail* – A coat of mail is worn by a battle warrior. It's made of tiny metal chains that are all intertwined together. It covers the warrior's shoulders and chest. Goliath's coat of mail weighed about 78 pounds!
- *His spear* – His spear was bigger than most men. That's a huge spear!

The Bible explains that Goliath was gigantic. He seems impossible to conquer. Sometimes when things go wrong in our lives, they seem impossible to conquer. The problems just seem too big. Can you think of anything in your life that seems too big to change?

_____
_____

ℬ. On a wall in your house, measure the height of 9 feet 6 inches. You will need help from an adult who can stand on a chair or step ladder to reach up that high.

Then, list your "giants," or your problems on paper and tape the paper on your wall at 9'6".

Think of the problems you are going through. Do they feel like giants? With God, they cannot conquer your life. With God, they cannot win. Dear sister, God your Father desperately wants you to know this. *That's why God went into such great detail about how big Goliath was.* Although he's big, Goliath is not going to win anything.

God gives us strength to battle problems. You just must trust God in the problem, remain in battle until it's defeated, and remember that God is with you throughout the entire fight. And when that fight, or that struggle, or that stressful situation is over, you'll be stronger in your faith and in your relationship with God.

The truth is that we cannot take care of the big problems all on our own, and we shouldn't try.

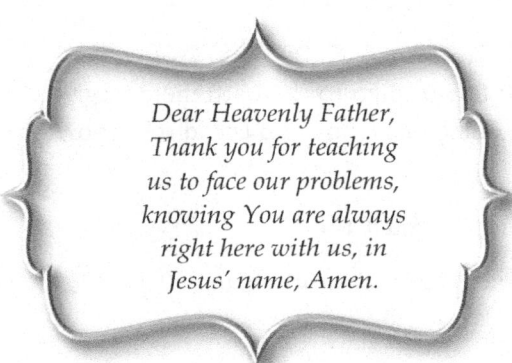

Dear Heavenly Father, Thank you for teaching us to face our problems, knowing You are always right here with us, in Jesus' name, Amen.

Lesson 2
Mom & Dad

A. Read **1 Samuel 17:8-20**.

Write a summary or your own thoughts of the reading:

_____

_____

When David's father Jesse asked David to go to the battlefield to give food to the army and see if his big brothers were doing okay, how did David respond? Check the correct answer:

_____ David said, "I'll go later, Dad; I'm really tired."

_____ He said, "Can't you get one of my other brothers to go? It's his turn!"

_____ He sighed and moaned and dragged his feet.

_____ He asked, "Why? But what about the sheep?"

_____ He rose early and left, as his dad commanded him.

According to verse 20, David obeyed his father. And this was no small command from his dad. Jesse didn't just command David to feed the dog. Jesse commanded his son to travel 10 miles south (which, by the way, David had traveled before to play the harp for King Saul) into a battlefield. David deeply honored and obeyed his father.

B. We have already learned that God described David as a man after His own heart,

and in order to seek God's heart, we have to read the Bible. It is possible that David had heard the words of Moses (Genesis, Exodus, Leviticus, Numbers, Deuteronomy) read aloud by a spiritual leader, and he hid those precious words of God deep within his heart, including Exodus 20:12.

$\mathcal{L}$ook up **Exodus 20:12**, copy the verse below, and hide it deep within your heart.

_____
_____

As you seek God's heart, how can you place Exodus 20:12 in your own life?

_____
_____

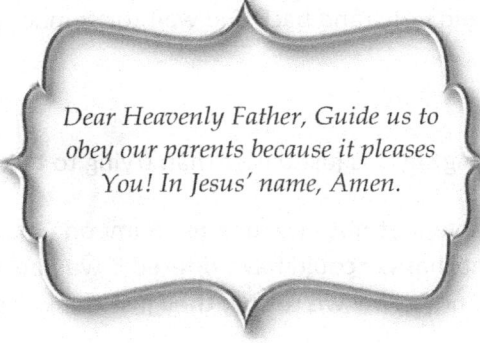

Dear Heavenly Father, Guide us to obey our parents because it pleases You! In Jesus' name, Amen.

Lesson 3
Hello!

A. Read **1 Samuel 17:21-30**.

Write a summary or your own thoughts of the reading:

_____

_____

David was social, and probably not shy. He took the time to approach the men of the army and greet them. He did not stand back and wait for someone to come to him first.

B. Oftentimes, behaving shyly is just easier than trying to talk with others. At three years old, it's understandable, but not at your age. Someone may still be left without a greeting or encouragement that *we* could have offered if we had not been shy. Besides, the people around us may not know we're shy; they just think we're being rude, or that we don't care about them.

It is difficult to approach someone first if you are not in the habit of doing so. It may feel awkward or uncomfortable; however, you are at a perfect age to start practicing and showing love for others. Be the first to greet someone. Walk up to the person, and just say "hi" or "how are you" or "what's your name?" It could be an opportunity to make a new friend.

Furthermore, the person doesn't have to be a stranger. Be first to greet your mom or dad after school. Be first to greet your principal, teachers, the janitor, and your church leaders and pastors. It's a great opportunity to do good for others and build your courage in social settings.

Look up **1 Thessalonians 5:11**, copy the verse below, and commit it to memory:

_____

_____

Lesson 4

You've Got This!

A. Read **1 Samuel 17:31-58**.

Write a summary or your own thoughts of the reading:

_____
_____

Reading the Bible is definitely not boring! Did you know that David actually cut off Goliath's head? You were probably never given a coloring sheet in Sunday school showing David cutting off Goliath's head. You are probably not even allowed to watch TV shows or movies that are this gruesome. God can entertain us like no one else. What's more, it's all true!

B. **The whole reason** why David planned to fight the Philistine is in the last statement of verse 46. There was something that he wanted the whole earth to know. What was it that David wanted everyone to know?

_____
_____

David had to face some obstacles along the way. . .

#1: His brother Eliab *was mean* to him.

#2: King Saul's armor was *too big* on David.

#3: David had *no weapons* except for five stones.

#4: Goliath *made fun of him* in front of everyone.

If David, who was after God's own heart, had to face obstacles when doing good, then we will surely face obstacles just like David faced:

#1: Others may be *mean to us* or discourage us.

#2: Our *plans may not work* out like we had planned.

#3: Maybe *we don't have what we need*, like money, to do good.

#4: Others may *make fun of us*.

Which of these four obstacles do you think slow you down the most from doing God's work?

_____

What's bigger – obstacles or God? _____

> *Dear Heavenly Father, help our faith stay strong no matter the obstacle, in Jesus' name, Amen.*

Chapter 4
Friends

Out of these billions of people in the world, a few are distinct, special people that you call your friends. They are a gift to you from God. What a wonderful gift to be funny and laugh with, to talk to and share your thoughts with, and to feel safe and happy with!

We also must remember that we have a responsibility as a friend to lead our friends close to Jesus. We help them make the right decisions, we comfort them when they're sad or upset, and we pray for them.

We also have a responsibility to walk closer to God every day. So, true friends will lead you closer to Jesus, will help you make good decisions, and comfort you when you're sad or upset.

Out of the billions and billions of people in the world, these friends are your refuge, a gift from God. Thank God for your friends. Praise God for your friends.

Never stop loving your friends.

$$\frac{me + u}{\heartsuit}$$

Lesson 1
BFFs

A. Read **1 Samuel 18:1-5**.

Write a summary or your own thoughts of the reading:

_____
_____

The Bible doesn't just say that Jonathan and David were best friends. We are told what true friends will do for each other.

- *True friends* love each other.
- *True friends* want to see God's will done in their friends' lives.
- *True friends* help each other make the right decisions.

Jonathan was to be the next heir to the throne, following his dad King Saul; however, Jonathan gave David his robe indicating that he was willing to give up this rightful kingship to see *God's will* be done.

How do we become true friends?

One word. . .

love

Lesson 2
How to Love My Friends

A. Read **1 Corinthians 13:4-7,** and write down a list of all the attributes of love:

- *protects*
- *kinds*
- *trust*
- *proud*

Circle the attributes above that you would like to see more in your own life as you love your friends.

B. Look up **Proverbs 17:17a**, and write the verse below.

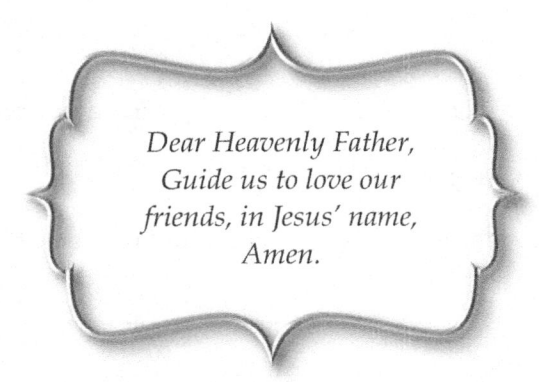

_____

_____

> *Dear Heavenly Father,*
> *Guide us to love our*
> *friends, in Jesus' name,*
> *Amen.*

Lesson 3
Instigators

A. Read **1 Samuel 18:6-14**.

Write a summary or your own thoughts of the reading:

_____

_____

Let's discuss these singing women. This is a great example of some of the music we should not be listening to. The women were congratulating *and* condescending!

Because of the women's careless words, how did King Saul feel?

_____

The words of the women caused jealousy, worry, and wicked thoughts in King Saul's head. King Saul must take responsibility for his own thoughts, but how do you think the women could have done things differently?

_____

_____

B. We must choose our words wisely. Your words can be powerful. Be sure that they are good, do good, and bring about good things.

Look up **Proverbs 15:4**, copy the verse below, and commit the verse to memory.

_____

_____

C. Please add **Proverbs 31:26** to your memory verses list:

_____

_____

_____

Chapter 5
A Strong Second

A couple looking for a new home drives up to a huge, magnificent cabin standing tall on the side of a mountain. The realtor with them explains that sturdy materials were used to hold this house upright, so it will not tumble down the mountain. Those unseen steel beams and wooden pillars have an enormous role in keeping the house looking great. All the while, they remain unseen.

There's an interesting verse in Philippians 2:3 that tells us to "let each esteem others better than himself."   To esteem others means to admire or highly value other people.

There's also an acronym for the word "JOY" that you may know: **J**esus, **O**thers, **Y**ou. We're to be last, but that doesn't mean that we're weak. As a matter of fact, it means quite the opposite. Only the strong can truly be second. Only the wise "seconds" will place Jesus first.

As a second, we have an enormous role in keeping others standing strong, and in keeping God exalted and first. Then, nothing tumbles down the mountain.

Lesson 1
Humility

A. Read **1 Samuel 18:15-30**.

Write a summary or your own thoughts of the reading:

_____

_____

In verse 17, King Saul is scheming and plotting for a way to kill David. He commands David to fight the Philistines in hopes that the Philistines will kill him.
In verses 18 and 23, David still highly respects King Saul. He believes that marrying the daughter of the king is a privilege that he did not deserve, even after King Saul tried to pin David to the wall with his spear!

B. What do you think humility (being humble) is? Discuss with a parent to help you out.

_____

_____

Everyone loved David. He was good-looking, a wise man, a fierce warrior protecting the country, and a great musician. Be that as it may, David remained *humble*. He did not regard himself as worthy for ***more!***

Being humble is ***understanding that all that you are and all that you have are because of God alone.***

Think of the wonderful things you have that mean a lot to you -- family members, things in your bedroom, things outside, your home, your school, your church, salvation, good friends, pretty hair, talents, popularity, intelligence, wisdom . . .
All these things are from God, and we need to realize that WE had very little to do with any of it. God gave *everything* to us! Like David, we can not regard ourselves as worthy for ***more***.

Thank God for all that He has given you and feel the warmth of being truly humble.

When we are truly HUMBLE,
we are THANKFUL;
then, we have JOY!

Humility ☩ Thankfulness = Joy

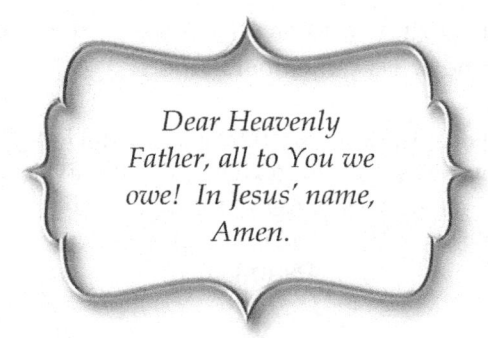

Dear Heavenly Father, all to You we owe! In Jesus' name, Amen.

Lesson 2
One More Thing, God... xoxo

A. Read **Psalm 70**.

David needs help, and he's turning to GOD! Another thing, David does not just say "Amen" after praying for help. He remembers others:

> Let all those who seek You rejoice and be glad in You;
> And let those who love Your salvation
> say continually,
> "Let God be magnified!"
> Psalm 70:4

Although David may have been worried, sad, and fearful, he remembered to pray for others and for God's glory.

B. Rewrite the prayer from **Psalm 70:4** *in your own words:*

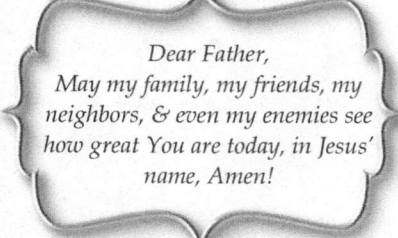

_____
_____
_____

> *Dear Father,*
> *May my family, my friends, my neighbors, & even my enemies see how great You are today, in Jesus' name, Amen!*

Lesson 3
The Power of Fellowship

A. Read **1 Samuel 19:1-7**.

Write a summary or your own thoughts of the reading:

_____
_____

King Saul and Jonathan may not have seen things the same way, but they do seem to have a good relationship. It's good that Jonathan knew that he could go to his father and talk about what was bothering him!

To keep a close relationship with your parents, share with them what is on your mind. You may or may not like their response, but you have strengthened the relationship just by talking to them!

Talk to your parents about this passage and let them know what you have learned from 1 Samuel so far.

*Dear Heavenly Father,
Help us to be honest and open with the parents You have blessed us with, in Jesus' name, Amen.*

Lesson 4
Please Understand!

A. Read **1 Samuel 19:8-17**.

Write a summary or your own thoughts of the reading:

_____
_____

Many times, when we watch something tragic on TV, we don't feel the sorrow that the people in the tragic situation feel. We just watch and see as outside observers. Most of the time, it's difficult to really understand what these people may be going through.

B. We just finished reading about David running for his life. What an interesting truth! To better understand what David was going through, it may help if we try to put ourselves in his shoes. Think about how his whole life was changing.

Pretend you are David, and write down how you feel, and what you're going through. Try to understand how horrible this must have been for David:

_____
_____
_____

> *Dear God, Help us to understand all that we read in the Bible, in Jesus' name, Amen.*

Lesson 5
The Comfort of Church

A. Read **1 Samuel 19:18-24**.

Write a summary or your own thoughts of the reading:

_____

_____

B. Can you think of someone in your own life like Samuel? Someone you can go to for God's truth and for loving fellowship? The church is not actually a building – the church is the group of people that are believers. It's where we find friendship, comfort, and answers. It's where we live out God's truth. It's where we give friendship, comfort, and answers.

Pray and ask God to give you a person from church that can be a mentor to you, someone you can rely on to pray for you and help you draw closer to Jesus. Then keep your eyes open: who is that person (or those persons) provided by God to be your spiritual mentor?

By the Way...
Verse 24 states that *King Saul lay naked all day . . . ? What?* One possibility is that King Saul was without only his royal garments. Another possibility may be that he became completely overwhelmed with God's glory.

Also, King Saul and his servants entered this holy place in Naioth, and prophesied, or focused only on God in some way. When we enter church, be prepared to be still and just know God, fully clothed.

Lesson 6
There's No Place Like Church

A. Read **Psalm 84**.

Copy verse 2 below and memorize:

_____
_____

Copy verse 10a and memorize:

_____
_____

B. In your own words, how did David feel about spending time with others that loved God?

_____
_____

Do you feel the same way as David, or not as much? _____

When I was a young tween, I didn't particularly want to go to church. I had a fear of being left out. There were four things that always helped me overcome my fear. Try these tips for yourself:

1. **Pray for my church leaders.** My preacher, my youth pastor, and my teachers needed my prayer to be filled with the Holy Spirit to show me God's love and truth.

2. **Pray for the other tweens in my group.** Sometimes, even at church, someone might be mean to us; however, praying for these meanies will help you remember that God loves them, and that they need prayer.

3. **Pray for our own hearts** to be ready to receive God's word, and to be ready to cheerfully and humbly serve others.

4. **Stop worrying.** Remember, everyone, including you, is a sinner at church, and that is exactly why we all need to be there.

My church today is my other first family. I love my church. My soul longs, even faints, for the courts of God!

David fled to a man of God, Samuel. Naioth was a village in Ramah; Ramah was Samuel's hometown. When David didn't know where else to go, he sought fellowship. Here, we learn something about David; he finds comfort in being with others that love God. He even wrote about it in some of his psalms.

*Dear Heavenly Father,
Show us the blessings of fellowship,
In Jesus' name, Amen.*

Lesson 7
Your Servant

A. Read **1 Samuel 20:1-11**.

Write a summary or your own thoughts of the reading:

_____
_____

B. Something important to remember:

When you see *"Your servant"* in the Bible, it usually means *"I"* or *"me."*
For example,

> *Your servant* is so glad that you are reading this
> Bible study that *your servant wrote*.

In other words, *I* am so glad that you are reading this Bible study that *I* wrote. I am calling myself "your servant." Your servant hopes you understand.

It's similar to how we respectively respond to adults with a "yes ma'am" or "yes sir." The way we respond shows that we respect the adult. It also shows that we are mature, well-mannered, and humble.

Look up **Titus 3:1-2**, copy the verses below, and commit to memorizing:

_____
_____
_____

David and Jonathan were best friends. Yet, they had a confusing situation going on. Jonathan apparently did not know that his father was once again seeking the life of David, and it was hard for him to believe that this was true.

So, David and Jonathan made a plan. Jonathan would bring up a conversation about David at the dinner table with his father. He'd then see how his father Saul reacted during the discussion.

Sneaky, weren't they? Now that we have established some basics, read on to see why Jonathan suggested going out into the field …

Chapter 6
All Those Around Me

What happens when you throw a pebble into a still, glassy pond? Think of the ripples created. The ripples are in order, one ripple waving because the one before it waved, just as God has arranged. There's an order to it.

So much in our lives creates this same ripple effect. Do you think it's possible that one of your family members is having a really good day because you took the time to smile, or to say "I love you," or to do something nice for him or her?

Also, do you think it's possible that this same family member has just told someone else something that has made their day better, and now that person will share their joy with someone else? Then, this person speaks to the ice cream man in town, and now Mr. Ice Cream Man is so happy that the whole town will get free ice cream tomorrow!

And,... it all started with you!

Lesson 1
Be a "Later"-Hater

A. Read **1 Samuel 20:12-23.**

Write a summary or your own thoughts of the reading:

_____
_____

In these verses, Jonathan spoke to David, who was hiding. Jonathan hoped that his dad did *not* want to kill his best friend. Then, David could stop hiding. But, how could they know for sure?

Jonathan had an idea. Jonathan planned some communication signals with David, kind of like code words. The signals would be made with a bow and arrows.

Jonathan would instruct a boy to run into a field where Jonathan would shoot arrows. *Where* Jonathan allowed the arrows to land would be an answer for David, who would be hiding and waiting for Jonathan's answer. Apparently, Jonathan was a skilled archer.

As David hid, he would know that he was safe and King Saul did not want to kill him if Jonathan's arrows fell *beside* the helpful boy retrieving arrows. If the arrows fell *beyond* where the boy was standing, then that was a sign to David that King Saul wanted David dead.

B. Jonathan was taking a risk in helping David. He was sacrificing everything to help his friend. EVERYTHING: his relationship with his father, his royal heritage, and his own life. Jonathan could have told David, "Look David, there's a big party tonight at the New Moon celebration, so we'll talk later. Oh, and, good to see you!"

Is that considered a true friend? Never. If we are good friends only when times are fun and relaxing, we're merely fair-weather friends.

To be a true friend, we must be *intentional*. That means we work at it.

Circle some intentional ways that you plan to be a true friend:

Pray for my friends.

Memorize verses with a friend.

Check up on a friend if she is sick.

Buy a small gift for my friend.

Write a letter or send a card to a friend.

Remember my friend's birthday.

Visit my friend

Invite my friend on a family outing.

Do a Bible study with my friend.

Call my friend on the phone.

Talk to my friend about our relationship with God.

Center God in your friendships and help them grow stronger.

> *Dear Heavenly Father,*
> *Help us to be a friend*
> *like Jonathan,*
> *in Jesus' name, Amen.*

Lesson 2
Jonathan

A. Read **1 Samuel 20:24-42**.

Write a summary or your own thoughts of the reading:

_____

_____

Can you imagine how hard it was for Jonathan to loudly exclaim those words to the young boy: *"Is not the arrow beyond you?"* (verse 27)
He knew David was listening, and now David knew that Jonathan's father wanted to kill David.

B. **Let's** concentrate on Jonathan for a moment. Throughout Jonathan's life, he knew he would be the next king. He probably often daydreamed of leading the army into fierce battles, or wearing the royal robe, or hearing all people around call him "King Jonathan." However, over time, Jonathan also heard about God the Father, and it greatly touched his heart. How do we know this?
Jonathan had plainly chosen God's will over his own plan of earthly royalty. He wanted to please his LORD. Undoubtedly, Jonathan also practiced obeying his earthly father as a child.
God wants *you* to practice pleasing Him over everything else, just as Jonathan did, right in your own home. He's given us a way to practice with our own parents.
Many times in our future, God will ask us to do things that may not fit our own schedule or plans. There are so many times when we would rather do our own thing than what our parents ask us to do.
If we don't practice obeying our parents now, it's going to be extremely difficult for us to obey our Heavenly Father later.

Here are a few things to look for in your obedience journey:

- Obedience never includes these sayings:
    "OK. I will in a minute."
    "Can I finish this TV show first?"
    "But I want to …"
    "How about this instead…"

"No."

"Why?"

- When obeying, our attitude should not grow worse.
- In obedience, we don't point our finger at a sibling, hoping to give them the responsibility.
- In obedience, we respond with "yes ma'am" or "yes sir."

Respect your parents and obey them cheerfully. It will prepare you for some big commands that your loving Father is preparing for you.

$\mathcal{L}$ook up **Proverbs 3:5-6**, copy below, and commit to memory.

_____
_____
_____

Lesson 3
The Truth

A. Read **1 Samuel 21**.

Write a summary or your own thoughts of the reading:

_____

_____

Doeg was close to King Saul, and they have probably known each other for almost their entire lives. (*Beware! – you will see Doeg's name again!*)

B. Our dear David... has lied -- the king did *not* send David. David was completely consumed with FEAR. He was afraid of what would happen if he told the truth. Now we'll never know.

But we can always know what will happen when we lie *(we've disobeyed God, a commandment, and we have made ourselves fake)*: we've added to the fear – fear of someone finding out that we have lied, and fear that something bad will happen.

You'll see, very soon, that there are bad consequences to David's lie.

Lying is a terrible poison that grows, taking us further away from the truth, until lying becomes a habit. Honesty always generates a greater result.

Look up **2 Timothy 2:15**, copy the verse, and commit it to memory.

_____

_____

Lesson 4
My Fab Fam

A. Read **1 Samuel 22:1-4**.

Write a summary or your own thoughts of the reading:

_____
_____

Take a look at the map on page 156 so that you can get a better understanding of where all these events are taking place.

David has nowhere to go, and he finds refuge in a cave. Verse one tells us that his family heard about it, so someone kept the family informed of what was going on with David. *"David has nowhere to go. He can't come home. They'll surely find him. He's hiding in a cave! . . ."*

B. Imagine how his brothers, his mom, and his dad felt when they heard the terrible news of David. Their love for David is shown – the brothers and parents find David so that they can be with him. What a loving family!
They paid attention to the needs of a family member.

Make a list of your family members:

_____   _____
_____   _____
_____   _____
_____   _____
_____   _____

Each family member has a need that you can help with. You can help build a strong family by recognizing the needs of all your family members *AND* helping them.

For example, if your sibling is studying for a test, they need silence to concentrate. If your dad is tired or stressed from work, an encouraging word or hug is helpful. Recognizing and helping with needs of your family will prepare you to recognize and help with the needs of others, wherever you may be.

*L*ook up **Galatians 6:2**, copy the verse below, and commit it to memory.

_____

_____

> *Dear Heavenly Father,*
> *Help us to see the needs of*
> *others, & in Jesus' name,*
> *help them, Amen.*

Chapter 7
Growing UP

If you were a flower, God would be the gardener. He is watering you every day. He's making sure that there's sunlight to keep you warm. He's weeding out those thorny weeds and watching you in admiration as you grow stronger and bloom.

Your growth isn't just in how tall you are or how big your feet get or how long your hair grows. Your growth is, more than anything else, strongest as you follow and walk closer to your heavenly Father. You grow as you seek His heart!

As you walk closer to God, you will find that your heart and mind will change wonderfully. Keep these wonderful changes in mind as you read through the rest of chapter 22 and 23.

Lesson 1
A Heart Apart

A. Read **1 Samuel 22:5-23**.

Write a summary or your own thoughts of the reading:

_____

_____

King Saul would *not* turn to God. Instead, he was disgusted with his servants, and was convinced that everyone was on David's side. However, he had one loyal servant. . . . Doeg! Doeg witnessed Ahimelech, the priest, give food and the sword to David. Doeg encouraged King Saul to be angry:

>"My King, I know who really hates you. Ahimelech!..."

B. Doeg encouraged the emotional King Saul to mass-murder men of God! In King Saul's emotions, he listened to the wrong person.

Have you ever noticed that when you're emotional, you say things or do things that you would not typically say or do?

Look up **Jeremiah 17:9**, copy below, and commit the verse to memory:

_____

_____

What does this verse mean to you?

_____

_____

Lesson 2
God's Input

A. Read **1 Samuel 23: 1-5**.

Write a summary or your own thoughts of the reading:

_____

_____

The "threshing floors" were the place where a farmer would take his harvested wheat and prepare the crops for cooking and eating.

B. As David and his friends hid for their lives, they were told of an attack in the village of Keilah (on the map). The Philistines, or "the bad guys," are taking the people's crops like barbarians. The families in Keilah needed help, and it touched David's heart. Before making any plans, David talked to God. Then, when it still didn't make sense to go fight while he was hiding for his own life, David asked God again.

WHAT DO YOU THINK, GOD?

What plans do you have for today, or for the week, or for your future? Write some of your plans here:

_____

_____

> *Dear Heavenly Father,*
> *We pray that we draw*
> *near to You, in Jesus'*
> *name, Amen.*

Lesson 3
Good Talk

A. Read **1 Samuel 23:6-13**.

Write a summary or your own thoughts of the reading:

_____

_____

When something funny, interesting, or bad happens, we may think of whom we are going to give the news to; and at the first chance, we're saying, "Guess what happened!..."

It may seem a bit different, but what if after a big performance, or after you see a hot air balloon in the air, or after having a really bad day, you just went straight to God and talked to Him about it.

For example, I'm very pleased with my vegetable garden this year. So, I talk to God about:

> "Dear Father. I know you know this, but I loved seeing all those sweet potatoes poking out from the ground. I can't wait to get out there and pull them up. What a great creation God! I love sweet potatoes! As you know, Annabelle is excited about helping me pull them up. Thank You for guiding her to be so helpful to her Mom. God, I pray I don't hurt my back pulling up the sweet potatoes..."

So, whatever may be going on in your life, talk to God about it. For example,
"Ballet practice was so much fun, God..."
"Dear Father, I can't believe how scary that roller coaster was!..."
"Dear Father, my brother won't quit picking on me...."

These are typically statements that we make to our loved ones, so how about to our Heavenly Father? The more we talk to God, the more the Holy Spirit will shape our hearts to be more like God's heart.

Look up **James 4:8**, copy the verse below, and commit the verse to memory:

_____

_____

Lesson 4
So Encouraging!

𝓐. Read **1 Samuel 23:14-18**.

Write a summary or your own thoughts of the reading:
_____
_____

Children can do some things better than parents, like using the remote controls, making a smore, or being fashionable. And I couldn't help but chuckle a little seeing how King Saul searched and searched for David, and then his son Jonathan just got up one morning and zoomed straight to David. King Saul would be horrible to play hide-and-go-seek with!

𝓑. Jonathan knew the needs of his friend, and he knew that his friend David needed encouragement. How do you know when a friend needs encouragement? Our *hearts* must stay in-tune to others more than to ourselves.

𝓦hat can you do this week to encourage a friend?
_____
_____

𝓛ook up **Hebrews 13:16**. Copy the verse below, and commit the verse to memory:
_____
_____

Lesson 5
He's Got the Whole World!

𝒜. Read **1 Samuel 23:19-29**.

Write a summary or your own thoughts of the reading:

__God   Help   Daved   seak__
  __wisdom__

This is action-packed Scripture! If you're not into good-guy/bad-guy stories, it's understandable. But there's something important in this chase that God wants you to see.

King Saul *desperately* wanted to find David, and the Ziphites were encouraging King Saul to keep searching. David was trying his best to hide; yet in verse 26, King Saul and his men circled around the area where David was hiding, so that David could not escape! This had to be a very intense moment. Yet, suddenly, a messenger arrived...

ℬ. Was it good luck? Or a coincidence? *Never.* As believers, followers, and sisters in Jesus Christ, let's all together, right at this moment, take the word *"coincidence"* out of our vocabulary! It's a pagan word. Nothing just happens as good luck or a coincidence. God's majestic hands are always there and in control. Here in chapter 23, God's loving hands worked in such a way that protected David. God's hands do the same in your life!

ℒook up **Colossians 1:17**, copy the verse below, and commit it to memory:

_____
_____
_____

Lesson 6
Nature Calls

A. Read **1 Samuel 24:1-16**.

Write a summary or your own thoughts of the reading:

_____
_____

B. In verse 2, the "Rocks of the Wild Goats" was in En Gedi, a mountainous area with rocky cliffs -- where goats lived, and named for the goats.

In verse 3, as King Saul "attended to his needs..." he had personal matters to tend to, and so he excused himself into a cave so that he could be alone. He may have been changing his clothes, using the bathroom, combing his hair, or caring for a wound. It just so happens that this cave that King Saul chose to use was the same cave where David was hiding!

David's friends advised David, "Here's your chance! Kill him!" Why did David choose not to kill King Saul?

_____

Look up **Romans 13:1b**, copy the verse below, and commit the verse to memory:

_____
_____

✝

Chapter 8
My Teacher

My fourth-grade teacher was the most wonderful teacher I ever had. She was always so poised, and I wanted to carry myself as she did. She also spoke so well, even when a student was in trouble, and I wanted to be careful with my words as she was. Of course, I learned math and spelling and all the other subjects, but what I really remember is her strong, amazing character.

As we read through the First Book of Samuel, we learn the events that take place as we are supposed to. However, there's more that God wants you to learn than just the historical events. We notice how David's heart seeks the heart of God. We take these words that God has given us and apply them to our lives today. We learn through these wonderful words from God how to be a woman after God's own heart.

Because what God *really* wants you to learn and remember is how close you and He have become!

Lesson 1
Be Inspiring!

A. Read **1 Samuel 24:17-22**.

Write a summary or your own thoughts of the reading:

_____

_____

When you overcome temptation and make the right choice, others may just see you -- others that God placed in your path, and these "others" become inspired by watching *you!*

It's easy to do what everybody else would do. It's predictable. Yet, it's out of the ordinary to overcome temptation, surrender to the Holy Spirit, and like Jesus, act in love. This kind of behavior inspires. This kind of behavior is how we can plant seeds of everlasting life in those that are lost.

Someone can always be *inspired*.

Look up **Matthew 5:16**, copy the verse below, and memorize:

_____

_____

> *Dear Heavenly Father,*
> *Guide us to be shining*
> *lights for You, in*
> *Jesus' name, Amen.*

Lesson 2
Tough Times

A. Read **Psalm 57**.

What verse spoke to you the most? Underline the verse in your Bible, and copy it here:

_____
_____

We're not hiding for our lives like David, but there can be times when we feel like no one cares or wants to be our friend. Stresses and worries feel heavy on our shoulders. In this chapter, God *longs* for you to know how to handle difficult situations.

B. God loved how David lived his life, because he lived with joy!

That's what God wants for you — JOY! Listen to how David found it:

- He **first** turned to God and asked for help.

"Be merciful to me, O God, be merciful to me!"

- David then realizes that this hard time in his life will end.

"...Until these calamities have passed by."

- David remembers and knows God will provide.

"God shall send forth His mercy."

God never expects you to handle a difficult situation without Him.

Look up **Isaiah 41:10**, and write the verse below:

_____
_____

Lesson 3
Giving

A. Read **1 Samuel 25:1-11**.

Write a summary or your own thoughts of the reading:

_____

_____

David's friends were going to meet the wealthy Nabal and ask for food. David and his friends treated Nabal's workers and servants very well as they worked out in the fields.

> Verse 3: *Caleb* was a mighty warrior for God hundreds of years before David was born. His life is in the Book of Joshua.

B. What was Nabal's reason for not helping David?

_____

Read **Matthew 25:35-40**. When we are helping others, whom are we really helping?

_____

Copy **Matthew 25:40b** below, and commit the verse to memory:

_____

_____

> *Dear Heavenly Father,*
> *Guide us to be giving of all that*
> *You place in our path, in Jesus' name, Amen.*

Lesson 4
The Beautiful Abigail

A. Read **1 Samuel 25:12-44**.

Write a summary or your own thoughts of the reading:

_____

_____

B. In verse 3, we learned that Abigail was

> *"a woman of good understanding and beautiful appearance."*

Here's what we learn about Abigail's character:

1. **She was dependable.** Others knew that they could depend on Abigail, and she would listen and help. How do we know that she was dependable? Look in verse 14. Who did the servant turn to for help? Abigail! He didn't turn to other servants, and he definitely didn't turn to Nabal. He knew Abigail would help.

2. **Abigail was giving.** Unlike her husband Nabal, Abigail "makes haste" and gave an abundant amount of food to David and his men. Look again at how much food Abigail placed on the backs of donkeys. How many donkeys do you think were needed for this much food? She was generous and giving.

3. **Abigail asked for forgiveness**, because **she was humble.** Although Abigail did nothing wrong herself, she asked for forgiveness because she was married to a man that had wronged David.

4. **Abigail had faith in God.** She explained to David how she believed he would one day be king because it was God's will.

5. **Abigail was beautiful.** Verse 3 tells us that she had a "beautiful appearance," meaning she presented herself as beautiful. Her hair was well-kept, she was clean, and wore presentable clothing. She showed gratitude for the beauty of being a woman.

God invites you to be inspired by His truth found in the Scriptures. He loves you just the way you are, but these qualities that Abigail had in her life helped her to be closer to God. He wants you to be closer to Him as well.

Place a check beside the characteristics that you would like to see more in your life:

_____ I want to be more dependable.
_____ I want to be more giving.
_____ I want to be humble.
_____ I want to have more faith.
_____ I want to have a beautiful appearance.

To help you see more of these things in your life, you must start in the right place. Look up **Matthew 22:37** to know where to start, and write the verse here:
_____
_____
_____

Then, pray to God about it. Write out your prayer here:
_____
_____
_____
_____
_____

Chapter 9
Closer & Closer

Today, think about God. Ask Him, "God, what do You love?.. What do You like?.. What makes You smile?... What makes You sad?..." Don't take any guesses. God's biggest answer is, "Let me show you." Then, I believe He will lead your heart straight to your Bible.

In a journal or in the back of this book, write at the top of a page, "Things I've Learned About God." As you read your Bible, pay attention to times that God is teaching you more about who He is. Make a list of all you learn about God along the way.

XOXO

Lesson 1
Night-Night

A. Read **1 Samuel 26:1-25.**

Write a summary or your own thoughts of the reading:

_____
_____
_____

Those Ziphites are tattle-tales, aren't they? King Saul starts the hunt again, along with three-thousand men*!*

Three-thousand!

All the men, including King Saul and Abner (King Saul's right-hand man), camp for the evening in the Wilderness of Ziph (see the map).

So, what does David do? He takes along his adventurous friend (and nephew), Abishai, to sneak up on all the sleeping men of King Saul.

Can you just imagine?...

> THREE-THOUSAND MEN ALL LAID OUT ON THE GROUND, OR LEANING ON TREES, SPREAD OUT ON A VAST AMOUNT OF LAND, SUCH AS IN A FOREST OR IN A PARK. ALL ARE ASLEEP, AND RIGHT IN THE MIDDLE OF THESE MEN LIES KING SAUL, PERHAPS SNORING.
> DAVID AND ABISHAI TIPTOE OVER AND AROUND ALL THESE MEN, CAREFUL TO NOT WAKE ANY OF THEM UP. ALTHOUGH DANGEROUS, THEY HAD TO HAVE HAD A SMALL GIGGLE INSIDE. WHAT IF ONE OF THEM ACCIDENTLY KICKED A SLEEPER IN THE HEAD, OR STEPPED ON A FINGER?
> DAVID HAD A CHANCE TO KILL KING SAUL ONCE AGAIN, BUT HE REFUSED TO HARM "THE L☉RD'S ANOINTED." HE JUST TOOK SAUL'S SPEAR AND HIS WATER.
> THE TWO MEN SNEAKED BACK OUT OF THE CAMP, AND THEN DID SOMETHING ELSE DARING. DAVID CALLED OUT TO KING SAUL TO WAKE HIM UP.

WHAT???!!! .... *T*ake time now to **thank God for the Bible**! Truth is absolutely amazing! Let's discuss this more in the next lesson!

Lesson 2
All for You, God!

Read **1 Samuel 26:25** (once more).

David wants King Saul to once again see how silly it is for him to chase David. Then, David says to King Saul something from his heart:

> "AND INDEED, AS YOUR LIFE WAS VALUED MUCH THIS DAY IN MY EYES, SO LET MY LIFE BE VALUED MUCH IN THE EYES OF THE LORD, AND LET HIM DELIVER ME OUT OF ALL TRIBULATION."
> 1 SAMUEL 26:25   *26:24*

Copy the verse above, or from your own Bible, and memorize:

_____
_____
_____

David was trying to please **God**; *not* King Saul, not Abner, nor anyone in Israel. David just wanted to please his heavenly Dad.

It seems nice to be valued and admired by other people, such as our friends, our teachers, our neighbors, or other people from our community. However, this can be a trap of glorifying ourselves. Perhaps we want to be noticed, or we try to get other people to like us. But then, God is left out. We don't need to worry about how other people view us. We need to strive to please God.

You will always be loved by God, so please *Him*.

We haven't seen our Father's face yet, but when we do, wouldn't it be nice to see Him lovingly gazing at us? Beaming for joy, so proud of His girl?

> *Dear Heavenly Father,*
> *We want to be valued much*
> *in Your eyes and please You*
> *in all we think, say, and do,*
> *in Jesus' name, Amen.*

Lesson 3
Listen

A. Read **Psalm 37:1-8**.

Copy the verse that spoke to your heart the most:

_____
_____
_____

*D*ear sister in Christ, please listen to the advice in this Psalm. David's words were inspired by God; therefore, these words are in the heart of God. God loves you, and He wants you to remember these words.

David had life-experience. So, when he wrote these words, he knew what he was talking about. Considering he loved God, he has good advice.

B. Choose to listen to and take advice from women of God – your mother, grandmothers, church leaders, or any other Christian women that God has placed in your life.

Be *discerning* with advice from non-Christians. From my experience, as a Jesus-follower, much advice from non-Christians EXCLUDES God. When the advice does not agree with God's word in the Bible, don't listen.

Many pop songs, movies, and TV shows offer their own way of seeing things. Their way may seem nice, fun, and even make sense, but it's wrong and leads to destruction. There's no good way around it.

*C*hoose a verse that you would like to memorize, and share the verse with a friend:

_____
_____
_____

Lesson 4
Wild Heart

A. Read **1 Samuel 27:1-4**.

Write a summary or your own thoughts of the reading:

_____
_____

Look on the map and find Gath. This is where David fled – to Philistine territory! *What was he thinking?* The first few words in verse one explains it: "And David said in his heart,…"
It was his deceiving heart!

B. Look up **James 1:14**, copy the verse below, and memorize:

_____
_____

Feelings and emotions come from our hearts. In anger, we may shout out unloving words. In sadness, we may think no one likes us. In happiness, we may think we are better than others. When we're emotional, our hearts deceive us, and our feelings can tell us lies. David was led by his feelings; so he feared, and he foolishly fled.

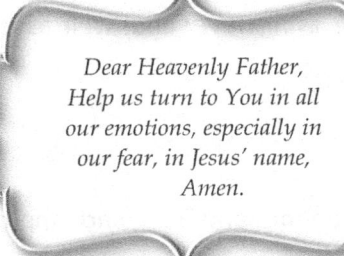

> *Dear Heavenly Father,*
> *Help us turn to You in all*
> *our emotions, especially in*
> *our fear, in Jesus' name,*
> *Amen.*

Lesson 5
Peace It Together

A. Read **1 Samuel 27:5-12**.

Write a summary or your own thoughts of the reading:

_____
_____
_____

B. Now, David is *living* among the Philistines, enemies of Israel.

Furthermore, he is *killing* enemies of Israel —
the Geshurites,
the Girzites, and
the Amalekites.
It's okay if you can't pronounce these words. These were enemies that defied God. King Saul never defeated these enemies. Even in David's weird decision to live with Philistines, he still feels pulled to fight for Israel. So, he's living with enemies, and he's killing other enemies. . .?

How will he explain this to King Achish of Gath? Well, David lies *again*! David tells the king of Gath that he is fighting *in* Israel... yet, he is actually fighting *for* Israel.
He is fighting a fight that King Saul wouldn't fight. David left no one alive, so that the truth could not reach King Achish. He killed everyone, this includes moms, dads, and children.
A bit too much drama, don't you agree? Lying *never* ends well, as we covered earlier with David. I'm afraid we will see it again...

C. God never commanded David to do this, and He did not approve.

Let's fast-forward into the future of David for a moment:
Later in David's life, when he is King of Israel, he desires to build a beautiful temple for God. However, God says to David,

> "You have shed much blood and have made great wars; you shall not build a house for My name, because you have shed much blood on the earth in My sight."
> (1 Chronicles 22:8).

TV shows have it all wrong – arguments and anger with friends or family aren't adventurous nor theatrical. They're hurtful, stressful, and even heart-breaking. We must strive for peace with those around us.

Perhaps a TV show with peace-making characters isn't very interesting, but that is how TV shows are different, and opposite, from real life. Making peace in real life is truly a pleasant adventure. Most importantly, we then have peace with God.

Look up **Romans 12:17-19**, copy the verses below, and commit it to memory:

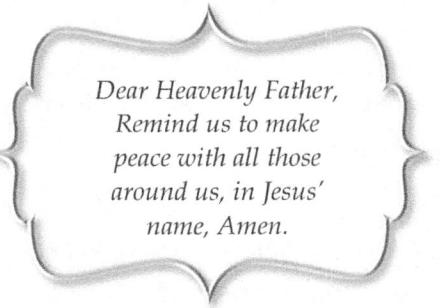

_____
_____
_____
_____

> *Dear Heavenly Father,*
> *Remind us to make*
> *peace with all those*
> *around us, in Jesus'*
> *name, Amen.*

Lesson 6
You There, God?

A. Read **1 Samuel 28:1-6**.

Write a summary or your own thoughts of the reading:

_____

_____

_____

B. God did not answer King Saul. Why not? Let's look to the Bible:

Job 35:12 explains that God did not answer the crying *"because of the **pride** of evil men."*

Proverbs 21:13 teaches us, *"whoever **shuts his ears** to the cry of the poor will also cry himself and not be heard."*

Also, **Micah 3:4** tells us that God will hide His face from the crying *"because they have been **evil in their deeds**."*

So, here are three possible reasons that King Saul did not hear from God: King Saul *had pride, he ignored the poor, and/or he did evil.*

At some time or another, we are all guilty of these things. We need Jesus to cleanse our hearts.

Psalm 139:23

$\mathcal{L}$ook up **Psalm 139:23,24**, copy the verses here, and commit both verses to memory.

_____

_____

_____

_____

_____

$\mathcal{P}$ray this prayer today and every day. We must come before our Holy Heavenly Father, the King of Kings, the Omnipotent, Sovereign God with a clean heart.

> *Dear Heavenly Father,*
> *Clean our hearts of sin so*
> *that we can come to You,*
> *our Father boldly,*
> *in Jesus' name, Amen.*

Chapter 10
Woman-Practice

You won't find a reality show on TV called, "Instant Makeover to a Godly Woman." Praise God that salvation is a gift from God and nothing we must work for, or *make over!* The bad thing about instant makeovers is that they can easily be removed. I can have my hair and makeup adorning me to feel like a queen, and the next morning, I'm looking like one of those rainbow trolls. God's grace is everlasting, but instant makeovers instantly disappear.

None of us wake up transformed into God-pleasing ladies with big smiles on our faces. Nope. Sorry. It's not gonna happen.

But every single day, God places wonderful opportunities before you to make choices that bring you a step closer to Him, a step closer to His will, and a step closer to becoming a Godly woman. Along the way, you'll need your instruction manual (the Bible), or you might get lost!

And if you practice now, you have the amazing opportunity to go to bed as a woman of God, *AND* wake up the same way! It's totally worth the practice!

This chapter covers some great instructions you'll need in your daily walk with God; and, as a bonus, it includes Bible passages!

Lesson 1
Don't Be Scared!

A. Read **1 Samuel 28:7-25**.

Write a summary or you own thoughts of the reading:

_____
_____
_____

King Saul visits a witch!
Yes, there are people that practice witchcraft. Not as in "The Wicked Witch of the East," but with just as dark of a heart. Satan loves them. They take all focus off God Almighty and draw a person to believe in something other than God's will. This opens a door for Satan and all his demonic friends. It is to be taken seriously.
Remember, our Heavenly Father is more powerful. God showed His power in the witch's house. He gave King Saul the truth.
And what does King Saul do? Does he fast for a closer relationship with God? Maybe bend down on his knees to pray? Does he head for the temple and the priest and ask for help? Or at least remorse for his sins and tell God he is sorry? Does he flee the witch's house, realizing what he was doing was wrong? No! He sits with the witch and stuffs his belly!

B. Read **Deuteronomy 18:9-13**, and write down what this passage means to you:

_____
_____
_____

C. Look up **Proverbs 11:27**, copy the verse here, and commit the verse to memory:

_____
_____
_____

*Dear Heavenly Father,
Keep evil away from us,
and guide us to seek You
earnestly, in Jesus' name,
Amen.*

Lesson 2
Set Apart

A. Read **1 Samuel 29:1-11**.

Write a summary or your own thoughts of the reading:

_____

_____

If you were a Philistine, would you trust David in battle? The man that killed Goliath, plus over 200 other Philistines? I don't think so. Not to mention, David would have been fighting against his own best friend Jonathan!

B. Think about that one year and four months of Philistine life for David. How do you think David interacted and lived among pagans (unbelievers)? Do you think he may have influenced a Philistine or two to trust in the one true God? Also, it seems that at least one Philistine would have wanted to kill David, yet he remained unharmed among them. Hmmm...

He did have his friends and some family members with him, which had to have been a great strength and blessing. All the same, David was surrounded by the God-less culture and customs of the Philistines.

Oftentimes, we are surrounded by people who may not be searching for God's own heart, either at school or around friends. David, as inspired by God, tells us in Psalm 1 what to do in these situations.

Read **Psalm 1:1-3**, and answer the following questions:

- We are not to walk in *whose* counsel? _____
- We are not to stand in *whose* path? _____
- We are not to sit in *whose* seats? _____

To do what everybody else is doing is easy; but as Christian sisters, God has planned better than the easy way for us.

♡ We walk in the way of Jesus;

♡ we stand on a path of doing God's work; and

♡ we just don't sit and get comfortable with unbelievers.

We're different. We're separate from this world even though we live in this world. However, we are not alone. Although it's not easy, we have each other!

Challenge yourself and memorize **Psalm 1:1-3**. It's long and may take two or three days, but it's God's guidance as you grow into a young woman. To help you memorize the verses, you may write the verses here:

_____
_____
_____
_____
_____
_____
_____
_____

Lesson 3
A Way to Help

A. Read **Psalm 5:11-12**.

What if the prayer in Psalm 5 said,

> "Let *ME* rejoice.....let *ME* shout for joy.
> because You defend *ME*...bless *ME*....
> Surround *ME* with a shield."

That sort of prayer is as selfish as anyone can get, yet we often pray only for ourselves and for what *we* want. Then, we forget about others.

Here, David is praying for *others that love God*. For *believers*. Like when Paul prayed:

> "...always in every prayer of mine making
> request for you
> all with joy."
> (Philippians 1:3)

And Jesus teaches us to pray:
> "Give us this day, our daily bread."
> (Matthew 6:11)

God *wants* us to pray for what we need and about what's in our hearts. However, God instructs us to also pray for *others*. The greatest way we can help others is by praying for them, and *being a helper is being a woman of God!*

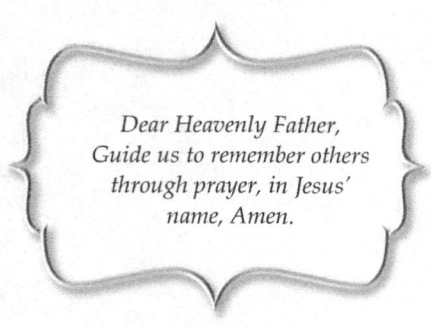

> *Dear Heavenly Father,*
> *Guide us to remember others*
> *through prayer, in Jesus'*
> *name, Amen.*

Lesson 4
Loneliness

A. Read **1 Samuel 30:1-6**.

Write a summary or your own thoughts of the reading:

_____
_____

David and all the men with him were in deep grief. Their children and wives had been taken away by the Amalekites, and the city Ziklag was burned. What's worse, David mourned alone. Everyone around him was angry with him.

In David's loneliness and sadness, *he found strength in God.*

B. Every single person in the world, at some time or another, feels lonely. Unseen, forgotten, set aside, or unloved. It's such a horrible feeling – I know (everyone knows).

SO, first of all, remember that you're not the only one feeling lonely. If you're human, you will have some lonely times.

Secondly, find comfort with your Father. Do you know how we close our eyes when we sneeze? It's automatic. We just cannot sneeze with our eyes open! Well, treat loneliness in the same manner: when you're lonely, automatically pray and pick up your Bible, as if you can't be lonely without praying and reading your Bible!

Achoo!

Will the loneliness go away? Maybe not. But something else will happen...

Look up **Philippians 4:6-7** and copy the verse below.

_____
_____
_____
_____

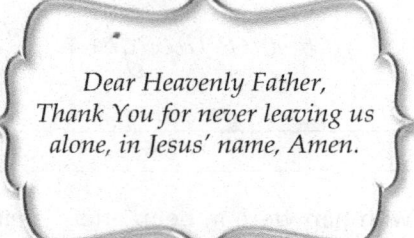

*Dear Heavenly Father,
Thank You for never leaving us
alone, in Jesus' name, Amen.*

Lesson 5
Something to Remember

A. Read **Psalm 8**.

A prayer that asks for *nothing* thinks only about how great God is.

B. Jesus taught His disciples that when we pray, we should begin our prayers by thinking of God, of who He is, and of how great He is.

> "OUR FATHER IN HEAVEN,
> HALLOWED BE YOUR NAME.
> YOUR WILL BE DONE
> ON EARTH AS IT IS IN HEAVEN."
> MATTHEW 6:9

It's all about God, not on our problems or what we wish God would do, or what we wish we could have. God *only!*

We have a great and strong Father. Our worries and wants are little and weak. God has all of our lives in His hands, and He can handle our problems. Let's focus completely on God, as David did, now.

Write out a prayer on the opposite page that focuses only on God. Include . . .

#1, who God is to you and to others (Protector, Father, Healer, Creator,...),

#2, what God had done for you and for others,

#3, what you really love about God.

Take time to think about it. Remember you are not including your own wants or needs.

This prayer focuses *only* on how great our Father is!

_____
_____
_____
_____
_____
_____

Chapter 11
Your Bible

I have an old Bible put up on the shelf. If someone tries to pull it out, it may come apart in many scattered pages. It was well used and is now worn. Obviously, it had a big impact on my life. When reading that old Bible in my twenties, I realized that it gave me all the instructions that I ever needed for life.

After you read this paragraph, pick up your Bible and look at it. Have you seen, through just the First Book of Samuel, how God has so much He wants to share with you, to show you, and to teach you? Are you ready to bend your Bible's corners a bit? Maybe acquire a dirty mark or two on your Bible from heavy usage? How about adding some underlines to verses that touch your heart? Which pages appear to have not been read too much? Which pages seem to have been read the most? Do you like to read your Bible? Will you make a commitment to read your Bible more?

If the pages get too tattered to read anymore, then that's quite a wonderful problem to have!

Lesson 1
The Believers

A. Read **1 Chronicles 12:16-18**.

Here, in chapter 12, we learn more about the men that were with David, and their loving words to David:

"We are yours, O David;
We are on your side, O son of Jesse!
Peace, peace be to you,
And peace to your helpers!
For your God helps you."

> The Chronicles give similar information as the Books of Samuel give. These books also give more information about history, from creation to Persian rule in Israel, which was around 500 BC.

From these words, we can learn how to be encouraging to other believers:
1. Remind them that they are important to us.
2. When fellow-believers are having a bad day, be ready to listen and help.
3. Pray for them.
4. Help them grow closer to God.

What believer and follower of Jesus Christ do you plan to love, listen to, help, and pray for this week?
_____

Write out a prayer for your friend here:
_____
_____
_____
_____
_____

Lesson 2
Our Helper

A. Read **1 Samuel 30:7-8**.

Write a summary or your own thoughts of the reading:

_____
_____

An *ephod* is like a vest or a smock. It symbolizes honor to God. The priests wore the ephod, symbolizing that they were "covered" in worship to God.
David put on the ephod to show that he was all God's and wanted to be covered in God's will. I imagine that he felt stronger just knowing he was wearing the ephod.

We have a similar strength that we can lean on each day – THE HOLY SPIRIT.
The Holy Spirit guides us to walk closer to God, to glorify God, and to do God's work. The Holy Spirit speaks through us and to us. We are given this gift when we trust Jesus as the Savior and Lord of our lives.

Ezekiel 36:26,27 teaches us about the Holy Spirit:

"I will give you a new heart and put a new spirit within you; I will take the heart of stone out of your flesh and give you a heart of flesh. I will put my Spirit within you and cause you to walk in My statutes, and you will keep My judgments and do them."

So, how does the Holy Spirit help us?

_____
_____

Lesson 3
Your Strength

𝓐. Read **1 Samuel 30:9-20**.

Write a summary or your own thoughts of the reading:

_____
_____

𝓑. Take a look at the map below. David left **Aphek to** go to his family at **Ziklag**. Ziklag was burned, and David is now hunting for the Amalekites that burned down their homes and took their families. They are headed **toward Brook Besor** to cross it. All this traveling in less than a week's time! According to the map, approximately how many miles did David and his men travel?

ISRAEL

Mediterranean   Aphek

Sea   **Philistia**
        (Palestine)

Scale
|-------------|
20 miles

Ziklag

Brook Besor

David is going constantly! These verses are packed with one struggle after another. No real peace. His whole family is missing. All the men that faithfully served him are grieving for their families. Two hundred men become so exhausted, they cannot go any further. Finally, David and four hundred men fight a brutal battle that lasted over twenty-four-hours.

What can keep us going when we seriously feel like we just cannot take any more? Either we are having too hectic of a schedule with schoolwork, chores, family time, friend time, and Bible time; or, we are overwhelmed with emotions, like nervousness, guilt, fear, sadness, anger, confusion, or loneliness. We are going, one way or the other, constantly! David *KEPT VERSES IN HIS HEART* as he continued through the treacherous days.

C. Read **Psalm 18:28-36**. Psalm 18:32

Choose a verse to memorize, and write the verse here:
_____
_____

Why did you choose this particular verse?
_____
_____

Share the verse with someone you love.

> *Dear Heavenly Father,*
> *Thank You for Your*
> *protection and Your*
> *blessings that we too often*
> *forget. Amen.*

Lesson 4
The Bad Days

A. Read **Psalm 13**.

Write a summary or your own thoughts of the reading:

_____

_____

Bad days happen! What's more, sometimes God doesn't answer our prayers just how we want Him to. David even said that it's hard to know that God is anywhere near when we have hard times.

> *"How long, O LORD? Will You forget me forever?"*

David felt it.
Moses felt it.
Jeremiah felt it.
Even Jesus, as He hung by nails on the cross, felt a complete separation from God. What a darkness *He* felt – so that we never have to.

God wants you to know that on those bad days, you can find peace by trusting Him and remembering that He loves you.

> *"I will trust in Your unfailing love."*

Cling to God in these times. Rest in His love. And even when your chin feels too heavy to hold up, praise Him.

> *"I will sing to the LORD."*

†

B. Choose some verses from **Psalm 13**, or maybe even the whole chapter, and pray these words to God. To help you remember the prayer, you may want to write the prayer in a journal, or you can write it here:

Chapter 12
Words of Life

Sometimes, when I'm reading my Bible, I feel like a flood of God's love comes over me, and I wish I could hug God. So, I take my Bible, place it to my heart, and hug it. Then, at that moment, I know that all of God's words from His heart are literally close to my heart. I love my Bible. Because I made the choice to read the words in my Bible, I gave my life to Jesus Christ. Jesus is the Lord of my life, and my Savior for all my sins. Now, through the gift of the Holy Spirit, I read my Bible even more; because in this life, in this world, I need God more. When I cannot find the words in prayer to speak to God, I just let Him speak to me by reading the words He laid out for me in the Bible. Although I've read them repeatedly, the words I read each morning are always fresh and new. They teach me as if I've never read them before.

I would not advise you to make the Bible such an important part of your life if I did not know undoubtedly how significant the Bible is. I have experienced its unmatched worth. I know, through life experiences, that the Bible is true. I know, through life experience, that it can give answers to problems and confusions. I know, through life experience, that to know God is to read the Bible.

Perhaps you think there could be another way to truth, to find answers, and to know God. I know, through life experiences, that there is not.

Lesson 1
"Stew"ing Over

A. Read **1 Samuel 30:21-31**.

Write a summary or your own thoughts of the reading:

_____

_____

And *this* is what it's like to search for God's own heart! David understood that everything belonged to God. Therefore, since absolutely everything belongs to God, all that we have is from Him. Since God is so giving, we should be giving as well, just as David was.

B. Read **verse 23** again. David gave thanks to God for letting the men win. All they had and all that was gained back from the Amalekites was a gift from God. David chose to remember and give to others. David was a good *steward*.

A steward is someone that has been trusted to take care of things. For example, an owner of a cruise ship will hire stewards to take care of passengers and other things on the ship. A wealthy landowner will have a steward that manages the landowner's money and land.

A steward for God works the same way. God has given us – well, everything! We are to be stewards with what we have.

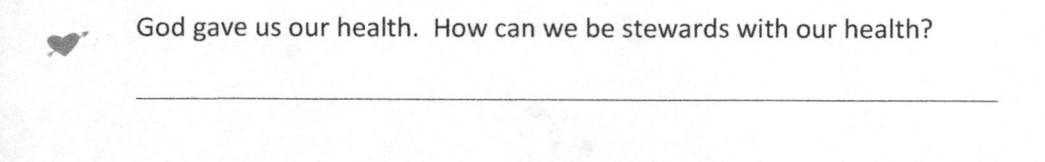

- God gave us our health. How can we be stewards with our health?

  _____

- God gave us our families. How can we be stewards with our families?

  _____

- God gives us nice things, such as books, clothes, fun toys, beautiful items in our bedrooms, beauty items, and so many other things. How can we be stewards with all these things that God gives us?

  _____

- Although you may not be making money by working, there are times when God gives us money. How can we be stewards with our money?

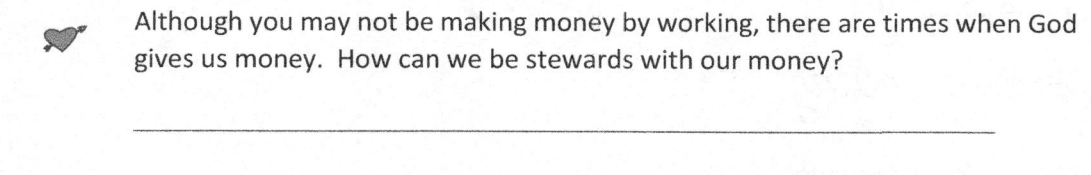

  _____

- God gives us time. How can we be stewards with our time?

  _____

> *Dear Heavenly Father,*
> *Thank You for trusting us*
> *with so many wonderful*
> *things!*
> *In Jesus' name, Amen.*

Lesson 2
A Sad Ending

A. Read **1 Samuel 31**.

Write a summary or your own thoughts of the reading:

_____
_____

B. And so is the end of King Saul. The way King Saul died mirrored the way he lived

-- Saul always took matters *into his own hands*. He never had total faith in God. Saul relied on his own plans. He dwelt on his anger and jealousy instead of on the power and love of God. Saul constantly forgot God because he constantly thought of himself. At Saul's last breath, he chooses, once again, to be in control. The Bible tells nothing of any final words to God, no prayer at all!

Saul was rarely *trying* to be bad. He never intended to be an evil king. However, he gave God very little time. At times when Saul did inquire of the Lord, Saul did not have time to wait for an answer. He took matters into his own sinful hands and made many damaging decisions.

Here is a question for some deep thought: do you ever live your life sort of, kind of, maybe somewhat, a bit like, a little like Saul? Thoughtfully (not quickly) answer the following questions:

Do you ever fear that someone may be better than you? _____
Have you ever thought you deserved more or better than others? _____
Have you ever been jealous of someone else? _____
Have you made decisions without talking it over with God? _____
Have you wished for praise and glory from others? _____
Have you done good works in hopes to be looked at, seen, praised, or glorified by others? _____
Have you left God out of a whole day? _____
Have you disobeyed God? _____
Have you spoken disrespectfully of or to a church leader? _____
Have you taken advice from someone who is not a Christian, be it someone you know, or someone on TV? _____

More than likely, at least half of these were answered with a heavy-hearted "yes." Like Saul, we often put ourselves first, and then we sin.
Only through Jesus Christ, we receive the Holy Spirit that guides us when these selfish, "Saulish" sins arise in our hearts.

So, as heavy as these questions may have weighed you down, remember that Jesus lifts those heavy burdens of sin off of us and provides His loving guidance. Thank You, our Savior! ♡

(This lesson is taken from my first book, From a Boy to a Godly Man: A Boy's Bible Study of David, because chapter 31 has some life-changing lessons for everyone).

> *Dear Heavenly Father,*
> *Help us to love & delight*
> *in Your will, in Jesus'*
> *name, Amen.*

Lesson 3
A Rough Start

A. Read **II Samuel 1:1-18**.

Here are some explanations in your reading:
- *The Amalekite man* stated that he killed King Saul – he is lying! He did, however, take King Saul's crown and bracelet, and then he traveled to find David, hoping to be congratulated.

- *The Book of Jasher*, or your Bible may say "The Book of the Upright," mentioned in verse 18, was a writing of details that parallel to events that are recorded in the Bible. It was a resource book, and possibly gave truths; however, it was not inspired solely by God and not added as a book in the Bible.

- *Tearing clothes* was a cultural tradition during that time to show mourning. Of course, we do not tear our clothes today when we are in mourning.

Write a summary or your own thoughts of the reading:

_____

_____

B. A very sad ending came for King Saul. The Amalekite man must have thought that he was bringing good news to David to tell him that the King was dead. He even decided to conjure up a lie and take credit for King Saul being dead. This lie cost the Amalekite man his life.

The Amalekite thought that David would rejoice at the news. Instead, as a servant of God, David grieved.
Here's a question for you: Was David grieving more because King Saul died, or because King Saul died without God?

Considering that David was desperately determined to know God's very heart, David grieved that the anointed King Saul died without knowing God Almighty.

Our hearts must also long to see others know Jesus. Whether it be people that we don't like, or the people that don't like us, everyone needs Jesus.

Look up **Matthew 9:37,38.** Copy the verses below, and commit to memorizing them:

_____
_____
_____
_____

What do these verses mean to you?

_____
_____
_____

> *Dear Heavenly Father,*
> *Guide us to have a heart for people that are lost, & guide us to build Your kingdom, in Jesus' name, Amen.*

Lesson 4
The Good Side

A. Read **II Samuel 1:19-27**.

Write a summary or your own thoughts of the reading:

_____
_____

B. David spent eight years hiding for his life, while King Saul's army sought to kill him. He is now free, and no longer in fear of being caught and killed. He had the opportunity to write a psalm of victory and triumph. Instead, he writes a lament, praising King Saul and his friend Jonathan.

David wrote wonderful things of King Saul, his enemy:
- Verse 19 states that Saul is *"the beauty of Israel"* and *"mighty."*
- Verse 23 states that King Saul *was loved* and *pleasant, swifter than eagles*, and *stronger than lions*.
- Verse 24 states that King Saul *took care of the people* in Israel, *clothing them in scarlet*, and *giving them luxuries*.

Look up and read **Matthew 5:44**. Write the verse below:

_____
_____
_____

Follow Jesus' command now. Think of someone that you consider an enemy, or someone that you just do not like.

Now, we are going to follow David's example. Write down at least five good things about this person:

1. _____
2. _____
3. _____
4. _____
5. _____

Way to go! You just took a step closer to God's heart!

me
+ u
♥

*Dear Heavenly Father,
Help us to see the good in our
enemies, as David did, and as
Jesus' commands, in
Jesus' name, Amen.*

Lesson 5
It's You, God!

A. Read **Psalm 67.**

Write down your **FAVORITE VERSE** *of the chapter:*

_____
_____
_____

This entire chapter is focused on thinking of God, and just praising Him. So many things happen when we completely focus on God – our worries grow weak, joy erases our sadness, we feel peace inside us, and we realize that everything is going to be okay!

> *Dear Heavenly Father,*
> *Let all the people praise You! Amen.*

B. In the empty space on the opposite page, draw a picture for God, or write your own prayer, or write a Bible verse in pretty letters, and have fun!

Chapter 13
Our Father

I'd like to share with you how my relationship with God first grew. It was actually through a Bible verse, Genesis 3:9 (which you'll see in the next lesson) that brought a flood of tears to my face, because I realized that God had been asking me that same question over so many years, and I had ignored Him.

On an index card, I wrote that question, "Where are you?"

I propped the index card beside my alarm clock on my nightstand. When my alarm boomed each morning, I reached for my glasses, feeling the index card brush my hand. Once my glasses were in place, I kept my head lifted from my pillow to see the words of my Father. I'd feel His love in my heart. Then, I answered, "I'm here, God." With a yawn and stretch, I started my day with prayer and my Bible.

I am not sure what happened to that index card, but I don't need it anymore. Each morning now, I rise very early, hungry to read God's words and talk to Him. I have learned over the years that if I do not start my day with my Heavenly Father, I feel spiritually dehydrated throughout the day. I want to be my best for Him each day. The best wife, the best mother, the best friend, the best servant. But I can't do this if I don't talk things over with Him first, and read what the Bible says; because there's so much He wants me to know.

Lesson 1
Here I Am, God

A. Read **Psalm 63**.

Write down a FAVORITE VERSE from this chapter:

_____
_____
_____

God wants you to say "good morning" to Him, and seek Him, and talk to Him all throughout the day. He loves you, dear sister; don't ignore him.

In Genesis 3, Adam and Eve fell into the temptation of Satan, and then tried to hide from God, their Father. All-knowing God knew where they were, but He encouraged them not to pull away from Him.

In Genesis 3:9, God asked Adam and Eve one of the saddest questions in the whole Bible. He asked, *"Where are you?"* God wanted to know where their hearts were, their thoughts, their regrets. He wanted them to talk to Him, because He loved them so much.

F ind an index card or small piece of paper, and write God's words,

Where are you?

P lace the question from God by your bedside; and in the morning, answer Him.

> *Dear Heavenly Father,*
> *May the reader of this*
> *book have a thirst and*
> *hunger for You, in Jesus'*
> *name, Amen.*

Lesson 2
David Makes History!

A. Read **II Samuel 2:1-3**.

Write a summary or your own thoughts of the reading:

_____

_____

Before David made a move, he "inquired of the LORD." He asked God first, and God directed David and his family to Hebron, which was just south of his hometown in Bethlehem. It's also just south of what will one day be known as "The City of David." This is a popular city name at Christmas time:

> "For there is born to you this day
> in the city of David
> a Savior who is Christ the Lord."
> Luke 2:11

In the City of David! Yes, David! Just think, the whole reason the City of David is mentioned in the New Testament is because David inquired of God! What if he had just made his own decisions, figured out what would be best for himself and for his family, and never even asked God about it? What if he felt that the mountains would best fit him, or the Mediterranean coastline? The Book of Luke would read completely differently, wouldn't it?

B. When we talk to God *first* about what decision to make, we will be blessed. We may not see the blessing right away sometimes. David had no idea that Luke would one day call Jesus' birthplace the City of David! Amazing things always, always happen when we talk to God about it first. Always.

What's going on in your life? What do you need to talk to God about? Do so now. You may write out your conversation/prayer here:

_____
_____
_____
_____
_____
_____

> *Dear Heavenly Father,*
> *Show us Your ways and lead us on Your path, in Jesus' name,*
> *Amen.*

Lesson 3
Hold On!

A. Read **2 Samuel 2:4-11**.

Write a summary or your own thoughts of the reading:

_____
_____

David wanted peace with the loyal followers of the late King Saul.
See the map to find where King David first reigned as King *(in Hebron)* and where King Saul's son Ishbosheth reigned as King *(in the rest of Israel)*. So, Israel is divided with two kings.

King David is not yet king of all Israel, but he is still indeed a king, *finally!*

B. Remember back in **1 Samuel 16:12**, God revealed to Samuel, *"Arise, anoint him, for this is the one!"*
David was possibly a tween, and no older than 15 years old, when Samuel first anointed him. He became King of Hebron when he was 30 years old.
That's at least 15 years of hungering for God's will! *Fifteen years!*

Look up **Galatians 6:9**, copy the verse below, and commit this verse deep within your heart:

_____
_____
_____

Lesson 4
The Struggle

A. Read **Romans 5:3-5**.

If we will be joyful in tribulations, then the tribulations will lead to
_____;

And if we will keep our perseverance and patience, God will lead and guide us, so then this perseverance and patience lead to _____;

And as we see God's glory and amazing ways that He can work through us, this building of character and new wonderful experiences in us will lead to _____.

And when we have hope, we won't be disappointed. God's word, dear sister, says so!

In our Struggles

Have Joy ⟹ Perseverance ⟹ Patience ⟹

Character ⟹ HOPE

B. David experienced so many struggles. Just think of all he endured: hiding from King Saul, the battles against the Philistines, being insulted by Nabal, living amongst the Philistines, losing his best friend Jonathan.
But he persevered. He kept his faith in God and became King of Judah!
How different may things have turned out if David chose to live his life without God!

There's two different ways of looking at problems:
1. These problems are too much for me, so I'm going down a different road of my own choosing!
2. These problems are too much for me, so I'm going to cling to God's hand even tighter!

Copy **Romans 5:3-5** below, and commit the verses to memory:

_____

_____

_____

_____

_____

> *Dear Heavenly Father,*
> *Some days seem hopeless, so*
> *help us to have joy, to stay*
> *close to You, & to obey You,*
> *in Jesus' name, Amen.*

Lesson 5
Let's Meet Our Contestants

A. Read II Samuel 2:12-23.

Who????

Abner
Commander of King Saul's army & King Saul's cousin.
He saw to it that Ishbosheth, Saul's son, would take his father's throne before David snatched it away.

King Ishbosheth
Saul's son, now king of all Israel except Judah.

Joab
Your Bible may state that Joab is "the son of Zeruiah." (David's sister - Joab is David's nephew.) Joab led the army for David. Had 2 brothers - Abishai and Asahel.

Asahel
Joab's brother. Relentlessly chased Abner to kill him.

Write a summary or your own thoughts of the reading:

_____
_____

B. Both sides believed in their kings, and they both felt the same about defending their king's throne. The result was blood and death.

While being chased by Asahel, Abner *tried* to reason with him. He explained that they needed to stop. Things would only get worse if one of them died. However, Asahel was focused on nothing else but winning, and it cost him his life.

Asahel would not *"look to the right or to the left."* In other words, Asahel had his mind set on one thing - himself, and no one could reason with him. Asahel only wanted to win.

One of the hardest times for us to see or even look for God's will is when we want things *our* way. And then, since we want something so much, we either disregard God's input, or think *our* way is God's way.

We all want things to go exactly our way. But the beauty in this life is finding loveliness and joy in the days that don't go our way. Learning that we were wrong about what God is doing is still learning something new about God! That's good!

Look up **Isaiah 55:8-9**. Copy the verse below, and commit it to memory:

_____
_____
_____
_____

Although God's ways and thoughts are higher than the earth, He still wants us to know them. All of them, and all of Him. ♡

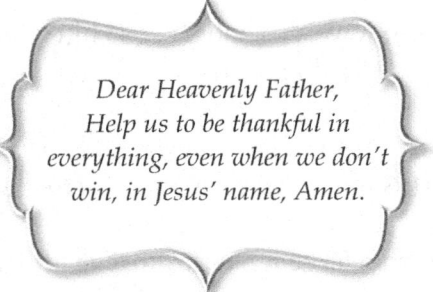

> *Dear Heavenly Father,*
> *Help us to be thankful in*
> *everything, even when we don't*
> *win, in Jesus' name, Amen.*

Lesson 6
A Message

A. Read **II Samuel 2:24-32**.

Write a summary or your own thoughts of the reading:

_____
_____

Although bitter enemies, Abner and Joab agreed to quit fighting. Many are killed, and both sides are undoubtedly sad.

B. Joab and Abishai lost their brother. Losing a family member is one of the toughest things in life to deal with. It's hard to face the truth that a loved one is gone. The sadness is normal, and it's okay to miss someone you love.

God promises a new heaven and new earth with new bodies to all that surrender their lives to Him through Jesus Christ. Here's the reassurance that God our Father gives us:

> Your dead shall live; their bodies shall rise.
> Isaiah 26:19

> Who will transform our lowly body to be like His glorious body.
> Philippians 3:21

If our loved ones that have already died could come back and say one thing to us, it would be this: *"Surrender to Jesus! He's real! Heaven is real, and Hell is real!"* They love you, and they want you to believe!

Be at peace with losing a loved one; fill your heart with love for Jesus.

Lesson 7
The Truth

A. Read **II Samuel 3:1-5**.

Write a summary or your own thoughts of the reading:

_____

_____

These verses give us some historical information about the culture in Israel during that time. Polygamy, or marrying more than one wife, was acceptable.

B. Since the Bible says David had more than one wife, is it okay? *No!* Read **Genesis 2:22**. This may seem like a silly question, but how many women did God create from Adam's rib? _____

Now read **Genesis 2:24**. Fill in the following math problem with numbers:

_____ man + _____ woman = _____ flesh

One man plus six women? No! Two men? No! Two women? No! God designed matrimony to be between one woman and one man. Therefore, David's lifestyle of having a different mom for each child, and having multiple wives, was not a reflection of God's perfect design, nor God's will.

Throughout the Bible, many men have had multiple wives. The result in every situation was struggles, turmoil, and stress, particularly with David.

Although this Bible study won't continue for all of II Samuel, the book continues with some heart-breaking situations that David had to endure within his own family.

How can we apply this Bible passage to our own lives? Well, there are many things in our society that everyone around declares as normal and acceptable, even leaders.

Dear sister, remain obedient to God's law, and stay in the Bible. Please read it daily.

C. Memorize scripture. Understand it, and live by it.

Look up **Psalm 119:11**, and copy the verse below:
_____
_____
_____

Memorize this verse, and as it says, hide it in your heart!

> *Dear Heavenly Father,
> Thank You for Your word
> so that we can walk in the
> way You have us to go, in
> Jesus' name, Amen.*

Chapter 14

Seek His Heart!

Every moment you pick up your Bible, it was already planned by God. As He inspired all forty authors of the Bible to write out His holy words, His heart leaped joyfully countless times as He knew that your eyes would see the words. He knew what you would think of His words. He knew which ones you would hide in your heart, and which ones you would think were boring. He knew which ones you would not understand, and how He would provide all you will ever need to know Him completely. To know His heart completely. To love him completely. Dear young woman, hunger and seek after your Father's heart!

Lesson 1
A Delight

A. Read **Psalm 119:1-24**.

B. Choose a verse to **memorize** and write the verse below:

_____
_____
_____

> *Dear Heavenly Father,*
> *Guide us to obey Your word,*
> *In Jesus' name, Amen.*

Lesson 2
Shhh!

A. Read **2 Samuel 3:6-11**.

To explain verse 7: A concubine was a female servant, and often an intimate "girlfriend" to the man of the house. Ewww! Ishbosheth accused Abner of committing adultery with Saul's concubine. We don't know if Abner was wrongly accused or not.

Write a summary or your own thoughts of the reading:

_____
_____

B. Abner wanted to strengthen the family of the late King Saul. Abner remained a loyal servant to Saul's kingdom. However, things quickly changed in verse ten, and Abner soon began serving the kingdom of David!
Do you know what it feels like to be wrongly accused? Perhaps you have been wrongly accused by a parent, or a sibling, or by a friend.
Many times, ladies of all age-groups are accused of doing something or being a certain way because of *gossip!*
Gossip is talking about others that aren't around to hear what is being said about them and to verify if the truth is being told. Ninety-nine percent of the time, it's not the truth. All those around that hear the gossip are being misguided. Many may join in, and you may feel tempted to join in, too, either by laughing or smiling along, or making comments that support the gossip.
Talking about others leads to someone being wrongly accused of doing something or saying something that the person, more than likely, did not do or say.
Don't participate! Walk away!

*L*ook up **Luke 6:31**, and copy the verse below:

_____
_____
_____

This verse is known as "The Golden Rule." Commit this verse to memory and share the verse with some friends.

> *Dear Heavenly Father,*
> *Help us to remember to*
> *treat others how*
> *we want to be treated, in*
> *Jesus' name, Amen.*

Lesson 3
Time for Work

A. Read II Samuel 3:12-21.

Write a summary or your own thoughts of the reading:

_____
_____

Abner *showed* a change of heart through his actions. He believed in the power of God, and he chose to be on God's side.

Having faith in Jesus Christ is the most important faith you can ever have. Now, if you have that faith, *do God's work!* *Show* your faith in Jesus Christ by doing His work.

B. Look up **James 2:26**, and copy the verse below.

_____
_____

If we truly have faith in Jesus then we will *want* to do his work. We will BE ON MISSION!!

Be on mission. Work in different ministries and allow God to guide you so that you can see where you can build God's kingdom the most.

Where have you served?

C. Choose some ministries that you would like to serve in:

_____ Caring for children in the church
_____ Caring for special-needs children
_____ Singing in the school chorus and/or church choir
_____ Playing a sport and reflecting Jesus on your team
_____ Playing an instrument and/or taking lessons

_____ Drama, art, music, or dance – bring Jesus joy!
_____ Commit to kindness with your siblings.
_____ Commit to helping your parents more.
_____ Choose a neighbor to help and pray for.
_____ Lead or take part in a girl's Bible study.
_____ Eat healthy & exercise; take care of the health God gave you.
_____ Write letters to show encouragement.
_____ Study your Bible carefully and equip yourself to teach others.
_____ Knit, crochet, or sew for someone.
_____ Dedicate yourself to your schoolwork, inspiring others.
_____ Start a "Prayer Journal," praying daily for all that you write in it.
_____ What other ministries are you interested in?
_____
_____

> *Dear Heavenly Father,*
> *Give us a strong desire to*
> *show others Your love, in Jesus'*
> *name, Amen.*

Lesson 4
Down Low

A. Read **II Samuel 3:22-39**.

Write a summary or your own thoughts of the reading:

_____

_____

David wept over Abner's death. David was a good leader and a good king because he *served*. Good leaders never feel that they should *be* served. Good leaders feel that they cannot serve others enough.

When we love and care for others above ourselves, we have **humility**.
You may have heard someone say, "How humiliating!" This would mean "How lowly I was brought down!"

To humiliate is to bring someone low. It's a verb and a horrible action.

To *have humility* is having an *understanding* in our hearts that *others come before us*. It's something special in the heart. To *humble* oneself is to have *humility*. Humility is necessary to understand that we need Jesus.

B. In each of the following verses, a box is given for you to add a name -- your brother, sister, mom, dad, neighbor, friend at school, enemy at school, whoever's name you feel the Lord may be leading you to write. After adding these names in each box, **read the verse aloud** using the names you wrote as part of the Bible verse.

Matthew 22:39:

"You shall love [　　　　　] as yourself."

Matthew 25:40:

"... inasmuch as you did it to [　　　　　], My brethren, you did it to Me."

1 Corinthians 10:24:
Let no one seek his own, but each one ⬚ 's well-being.

Philippians 2:3,4
Let nothing be done through selfish ambition or conceit, but in lowliness of mind let each esteem better than himself. ⬚

Choose one of the four verses to copy as written in your own Bible, and commit the verse to memory:
_____
_____
_____

*Dear Heavenly Father,
Turn our hearts to love others as deeply as You do, in Jesus' name,
Amen.*

Lesson 5
The Two Paths

A. Read **2 Samuel 4**.

Write a summary or your own thoughts of the reading:

_____
_____

Do not eat meatloaf while reading this chapter, with stabbings and body parts being cut off. Yuck!

Two bad guys, named Rechab and Baanah, are also brothers. They killed the king of Israel, King Ishbosheth, Saul's son.

Do you think these two brothers did everything together growing up? More than likely, yes. Siblings should be our best friends.

It's possible that one brother brought up the idea of killing King Ishbosheth. Perhaps the other brother didn't really want to, but went along with it anyway. After all, they were brothers. They did everything together.

What if one of the brothers had made the right choice, and said, "No way! I'm not killing King Ishbosheth!"

Perhaps this could have led the other brother to rethink how foolish it was to murder the king. However, neither would take a stand for righteousness, and their sin killed the king. Eventually, their sin killed the both of them as well.

B. When a friend or sibling wants to make a sinful choice, you *must*, in love, choose not to be involved. Also, try to guide them away from their sinful choice.

Look up **Philippians 1:27**, copy the verse below and commit the verse to memory:

_____
_____
_____

Share this verse with a good friend and a sibling.

*Dear Heavenly Father,
Help us to make the choice to
obey You, & give us strength
to choose righteousness, in
Jesus' name, Amen.*

Lesson 6
The Journey Continues

𝒜. Read **2 Samuel 5:1-10**.

Write a summary or your own thoughts of the reading:

_____
_____

There was a time in David's life when he had thoughts just like you. He had no idea what was going to happen in his future. He was often afraid, sometimes lonely, angry, hungry, and confused. Yet, he was determined to find out what was in the very heart of our heavenly Father.

David loved God and was amazed by God. David knew he could trust God, talk to God, and he wanted to make God proud!

(*Now, place your name in the place of David's name in the sentence above. Write the sentence with your name in a journal.*)

ℬ. Perhaps once King David was finally king, he thought back about how things used to be. From a shepherd boy, to a harpist, to a giant-slayer, and then the King's enemy. David did not forget all that had happened in his life, because he wrote it down. We can read all his writings in the Book of Psalms. David explains his hard days and his good days. *He wrote it down!*

𝒦eep a journal to help you search after God's own heart. In your journal, as days go by, you can include any and/or all the following:

1. Write a thank you letter to God.
2. Write down what you think of God.
3. Write down a verse you have read in the Bible that you would like to remember.

4. Write a prayer request to God.
5. Make a list of blessings from God.
6. Write out memory verses.
7. Write down something someone said to you that you would like to remember.
8. Write down how you would like God to help you grow.
9. Write down a list of reasons why you love God.
10. Write down an answer that God is giving you.
11. Write a prayer about someone you have been thinking about.
12. Write down a Bible verse that confuses you, and why.
13. Thank God for your parents, particularly your dad, in writing.
14. Write about an event where you knew God was there.
15. Write down some things you heard in a sermon that you want to remember.
16. Write down what you hope your future will be like.
17. Write down your wishes and dreams.
18. Write down ways you are growing closer to God.
19. Write a list of things and people to pray for.
20. Write about your favorite missionary.
21. Write about another Christian you look up to, and that you would like to be like.
22. Write about your future husband.
23. Write out the words to a praise song you really like.
24. Write a list of things you would like to do for God.
25. Write out temptations you have had, and ask God to help you overcome them.
26. Write questions you have for God.

Make sure you include the date in each of your writing, so that when you go back and read it one day in the future, you can better recall the time-period.

As all of David's life was going on, God had *you* in his heart. Now that you have read about the life of David, what do you think God wants you to know about God Himself?

_____
_____
_____

*D*o you want to seek after God's heart?

_____
_____

Have you accepted, without any doubt, that you have made the choice to take the gift of forgiveness, given by Jesus? _____

Have you on this day and throughout this week made Jesus Christ the Lord of your life? _____

Do you want to seek after God's own heart? _____

After reading through most of the life of David, do you see how serving God is adventurous, courageous, and rewarding? _____

C. Seek God first each day, dear sister! Look up **Matthew 6:33**, copy the verse below, and commit the verse to memory:

_____
_____
_____

Dear young lady,
I pray that you hunger to know the heart of God more. I pray that you make decisions that please God. Please do not worry, and know that your heavenly Father has a plan for you beyond your imagination. Love Him with your every breath! Thirst for each and every word in your Bible!

All my God-given love,
Katy Foster

Extra Room For YOU:

Bible Memory Verses

Psalm 119:18 Open my eyes, that I may see Wondrous things from Your law.

Psalm 119:50 This is my comfort in my affliction, For Your word has given me life.

2 Corinthians 4:6 For it is the God who commanded light to shine out of darkness, who has shone in our hearts to give the light of the knowledge of the glory of God in the face of Jesus Christ.

1 Samuel 16:7b "For the LORD does not see as man sees; for man looks at the outward appearance, but the LORD looks at the heart."

1 Timothy 4:12 Let no one despise your youth, but be an example to the believers in word, in conduct, in love, in spirit, in faith, in purity.

Psalm 115:1 Not unto us, O LORD, not unto us, But to Your name give glory, Because of Your mercy, Because of Your truth.

Exodus 20:12 Honor your father and your mother, that your days may be long upon the land which the LORD your God is giving you.

1 Thessalonians 5:11 Therefore comfort each other and edify one another, just as you also are doing.

Proverbs 17:17a A friend loves at all times.

Proverbs 15:4 A wholesome tongue is a tree of life, but perverseness in it breaks the spirit.

Psalm 70:4 Let all those who seek you rejoice and be glad in You, and let those who love Your salvation say continually, "Let God be magnified!"

Psalm 84:2 My soul longs, yes, even faints for the courts of the LORD; My heart and my flesh cry out for the living God.

Psalm 84:10a For a day in Your courts is better than a thousand.

Titus 3:1-2 Remind them to be subject to rulers and authorities, to obey, to be ready for every good work, to speak evil of no one, to be peaceable, gentle, showing all humility to all men.

Proverbs 3:5-6 Trust in the LORD with all your heart, and lean not on your own understanding. In all your ways, acknowledge Him, and He shall direct your paths.

2 Timothy 2:15 Be diligent to present yourself approved to God, a worker who does not need to be ashamed, rightly dividing the word of truth.

Galatians 6:2 Bear one another's burdens, and so fulfill the law of Christ.

Jeremiah 17:9 The heart is deceitful above all things, and desperately wicked; who can know it?

James 4:8a Draw near to God and He will draw near to you.

Hebrews 13:16 But do not forget to do good and to share, for with such sacrifices God is well pleased.

Colossians 1:17 And He is before all things and in Him all things consist.

Romans 13:1 Let every soul be subject to the governing authorities. For there is no authority except from God, and the authorities that exist are appointed by God.

Matthew 5:16 Let your light so shine before men, that they may see your good works and glorify your Father in heaven.

Isaiah 41:10 Fear not, for I am with you; Be not dismayed, for I am your God. I will strengthen you. Yes, I will help you. I will uphold you with My righteous right hand.

Matthew 25:40b "Assuredly, I say to you, inasmuch as you did it to one of the least of these My brethren, you did it to Me."

1 Samuel 26:25b "So let my life be valued much in the eyes of the LORD, and let Him deliver me out of all tribulation."

Romans 12:17-18 Repay no one evil for evil. Have regard for good things in the sight of all men. If it is possible, as much as depends on you, live peaceably with all men.

Psalm 139:23,24 Search me, O God, and know my heart; Try me, and know my anxieties; And see if there is any wicked way in me, and lead me in the way everlasting.

Proverbs 11:27 He who earnestly seeks good finds favor, but trouble will come to him who seeks evil.

Philippians 4:6-7 Be anxious for nothing, but in everything, by prayer and supplication, with thanksgiving, let your requests be made known to God; and the peace of God, which surpasses all understanding, will guard your hearts and minds through Christ Jesus.

Matthew 9:37, 38 Then He said to His disciples, "The harvest truly is plentiful, but the laborers are few. Therefore, pray the Lord of the harvest to send out laborers into His harvest."

Matthew 5:44 "But I say to you, love your enemies, bless those who curse you, do good to those who hate you, and pray for those who spitefully use you and persecute you."

Galatians 6:9 And let us not grow weary while doing good, for in due season we shall reap if we do not lose heart.

1 Thessalonians 5:18 In everything give thanks; for this is the will of God in Christ Jesus for you.

Philippians 4:8 Finally, brethren, whatever things are true, whatever things are noble, whatever things are just, whatever things are pure, whatever things are lovely, whatever things are of good report, if there is any virtue and if there is anything praiseworthy – meditate on these things.

Psalm 119:24 Your testimonies also are my delight and my counselors.

Luke 6:31 And just as you want men to do to you, you also do to them likewise.

James 2:26 For as the body without the spirit is dead, so faith without works is dead also.

Matthew 22:39 "And the second is like it: 'You shall love your neighbor as yourself.' "

1 Corinthians 10:24 Let no one seek his own, but each one the other's well-being.

Philippians 2:3,4 Let nothing be done through selfish ambition or conceit, but in lowliness of mind let each esteem others better than himself. Let each of you look out not only for his own interests, but also for the interest of others.

Matthew 6:33 "But seek first the kingdom of God and His righteousness, and all these things shall be added to you."

Matthew 22:37 Jesus said to him, "You shall love the LORD your God with all your heart, with all your soul, and with all your mind."

Proverbs 31:26 She opens her mouth with wisdom, and on her tongue is the law of kindness.

Isaiah 55:8,9 "For My thoughts are not your thoughts, nor are your ways My ways," says the LORD, "for as the heavens are higher than the earth, so are My ways higher than your ways, and My thoughts higher than your thoughts."

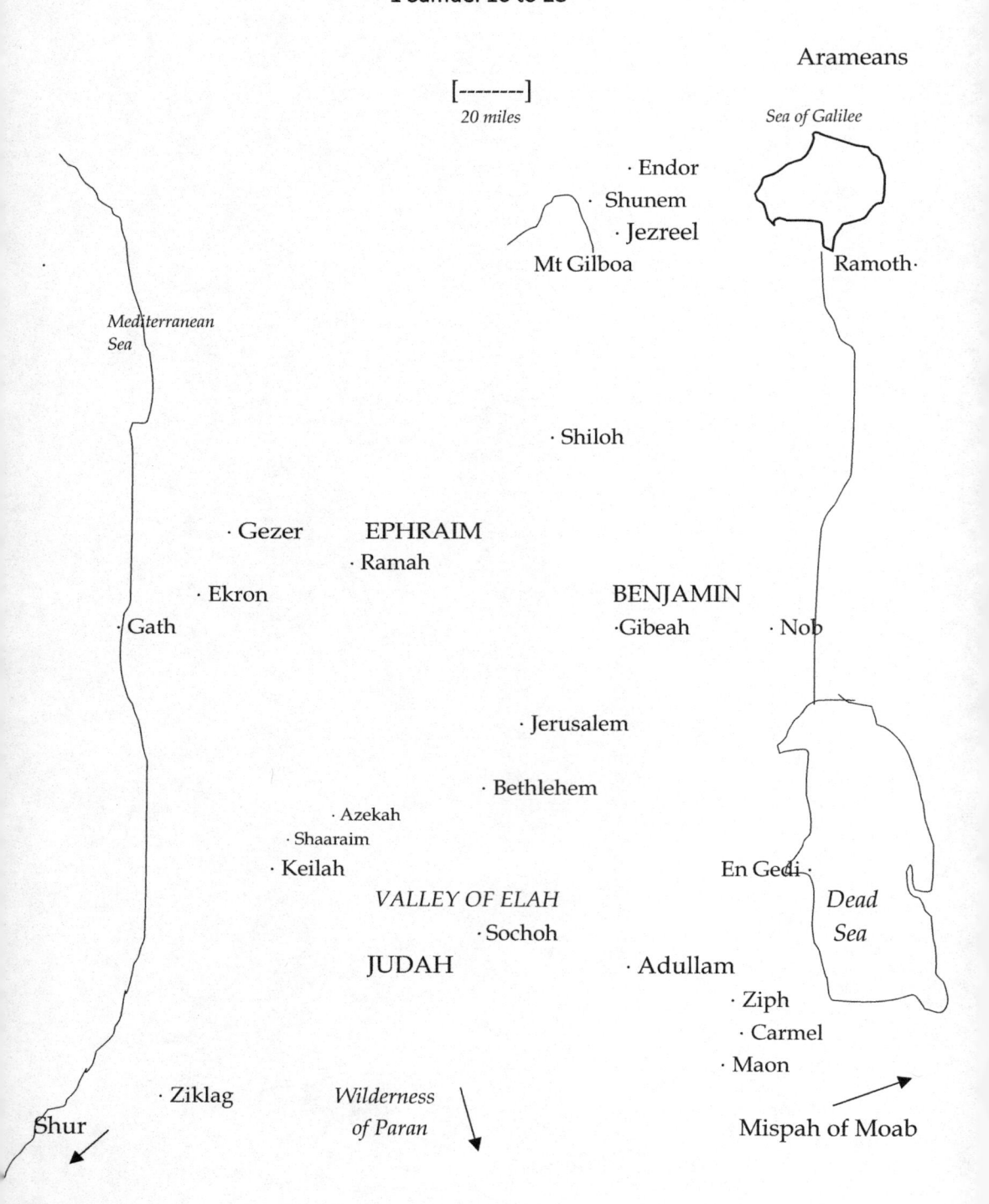

Map of Israel & Judah
1 Samuel 16 to 28

Map of Israel & Judah
1 Samuel 29, 30 & 31; 2 Samuel 1-5

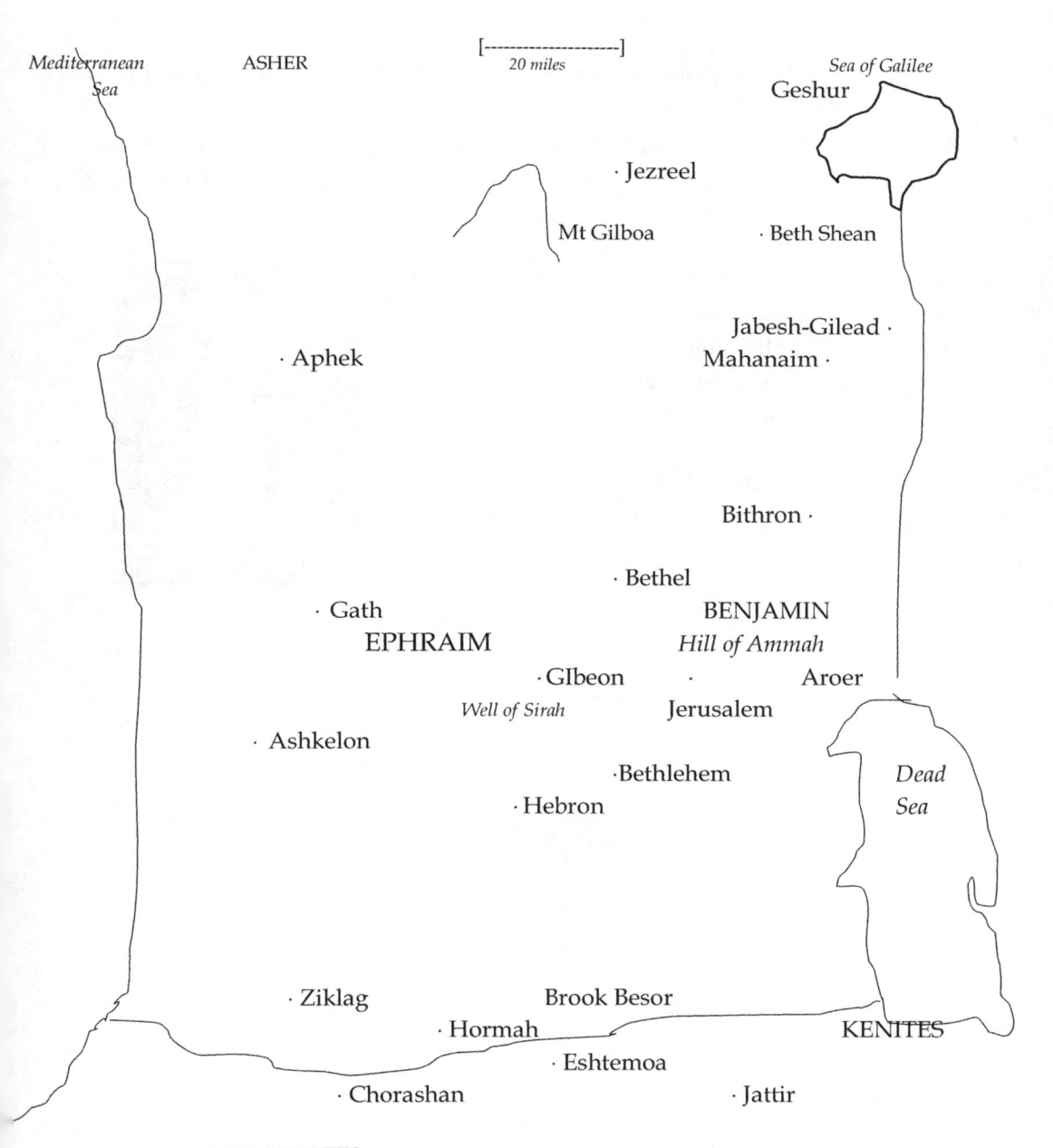

About the Author

Katy Foster resides in Flowery Branch Georgia, with her husband Christopher and three children. Chris and Katy have written three Bible studies together for tween and teenage boys, including *From a Boy to a Godly Man: A Boy's Bible Study of David*; secondly, *A Boy's Bible Study of Joseph*; and most recent for teenage young men, *A Boy's Bible Study of Jesus*.

A King David Kind of Girl: A Girl's Bible Study is Katy Foster's first Bible study for girls, written with her two daughters in mind, ages 11 and 12 at the time of publication.
Katy has been homeschooling over eleven years and has written much of her children's curriculum for every subject, keeping in step with her passion for writing and teaching.
As a member of Faithwriters, Katy also writes devotonals and Christian short stories. She enjoys teaching, reading, writing, and all outdoor activities.

Bible Study books by Katy Foster

From a Boy to a Godly Man: A Boy's Bible Study of David

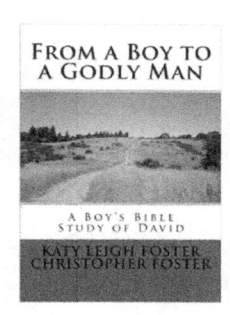

From a Boy to a Godly Man: A Boy's Bible Study of Joseph

From a Boy to a Godly Man: A Boy's Bible Study of Jesus

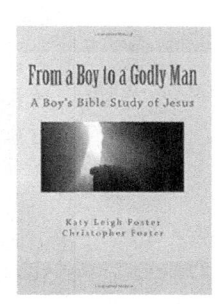

Available on Amazon on all other major online stores.

Made in the USA
Columbia, SC
17 November 2023